CULTURE DECKS DECODED

BRETTON PUTTER

"Corporate culture is the only sustainable competitive advantage that is completely within the control of the entrepreneur."

—David Cummings, co-founder, Pardot

ABOUT THE AUTHOR

Bretton Putter is the founder & CEO of CultureGene a company culture consultancy helping high-growth technology companies to prepare for and execute at scale. Prior to founding CultureGene Brett spent 16 years as the Managing Partner of a leading executive search firm where he successfully completed CxO, VP and Director level searches for over 400 start-up and high-growth technology companies in the UK, US and across EMEA. Brett is an investor in Seedcamp funds I, II, III & IV and an investor in, and adviser to a number of high-growth startups. Brett is publishing his second book The Culture Gene: Leadership and Culture Development Lessons from High-growth Companies during the latter part of 2018.

This handbook is dedicated to my *ICE* family.

www.icelist.eu

Special shout out to Andy Young, Rikke Rosenlund, Tom Ball and Dylan Bourguignon for pushing me to start the CultureGene blog. Thanks also to the ICE founders Alex Hoye, Peter Ward, Andrew Scott and Natasha Guerra, and finally to Alicia Navarro the truly remarkable co-founder of Skimlinks who agreed to be the first CEO to be interviewed for my blog.

Thanks also to my editor Angela Panayotopolus, copywriter Elloa Atkinson and designer Phillip Gessert.

"This handbook is required reading for every founder, CEO and HR leader."

Andrew J. Scott, Partner 7 Percent Ventures

"This handbook is a godsend to anyone who has spent any time trying to write their own culture deck."

Frank Johnson Director, Allied Crane Hire

"Progress comes from standing on the shoulders of giants. Brett supplies the ladder with this excellent handbook."

Rob Williams CEO, Plumb Guarantee

"A culture deck/code/manual/manifesto (call it what you want) is table stakes when it comes to winning the war for talent. This handbook is your entry."

Michael Papageorge Founder & Managing Director, IT Energy

"This handbook made me realize how much more I need to do to differentiate our company in a hugely competitive talent market."

Neal Vance, Cutterline

"This handbook is brilliant! Brett really simplifies the process of creating a culture deck. The slides he has chosen give a fascinating insight into the culture of the companies he has chosen."

Adam Posma CEO, ClubCollect

"Using this handbook to help create your culture deck will save you hours of time and ensure that it resonates with your target audience."

Ed Spiegel CEO, Dr Footprint

"Every high growth startup Founder should read this handbook. Using his 17 years of experience, Brett has put together a framework for Founders to build great company cultures, and consequently great companies, from day one."

Romanie Thomas CEO, JuggleJobs

"The fact that 9 out of 10 founders haven't done anything about their company culture doesn't surprise me, as I've never had a conversation with another founder about a culture deck, but having read this it makes me wonder why and has prompted me to get to work on my own!"

Dan McGuire CEO, cube19

"Culture is such an important part of the teams that I have built, I wish that I had read this handbook years ago."

Ivailo Jordanov, CEO Printastic

"Reading the content of these slides is a real eye opener. You get an immediate sense of each company's culture."

Bronwen Loubser, CEO Frames@53

"I've admired Brett's take on the importance of culture for years now, and have turned to him several times for counsel during turning points in my firm's growth. If you want invaluable guidance and insight into how to craft an effective culture deck for your company, this handbook is for you."

Colette Ballou CEO, Ballou PR

"If the Netflix deck is the most important document to come out of Silicon Valley, this must be the most important document to come out of Silicon Roundabout."

Natasha Guerra, CEO Runway East

"Culture is critical to the success of high growth startups. Culture Decks Decoded provides a comprehensive evaluation of some of the world's most successful company cultures, and a playbook for startup founders and aspiring entrepreneurs on this critical subject. An essential read on how to create an excellent culture deck for your business.'

Tom Impallomeni, Co-Founder & CEO Tribe XR

"I've been lucky enough to work with over a 1000 of the UK's most successful entrepreneurs. What they all share is an uncanny ability to attract and retain the very best talent. And they do that by obsessing over culture, vision, mission and values. Brett has written a brilliant blueprint on how to communicate and leverage yours by assimilating the best of the best culture decks in one place. Buy this handbook and ensure you build the culture, team and the success you deserve!"

Duncan Cheatle, founder The Supper Club

"This handbook is a game changer."

Alex Hoye, CEO Faction

"When should a startup start working actively on defining its culture? Since I co-founded Reedsy in 2014, this question has always puzzled me: how can I define the culture of a company when it's just me and my co-founders? When is your culture starting to appear and then what should you do so it evolves positively? How do I make sure it's not all fake? Culture Decks Decoded is a great read for entrepreneurs who are not just looking at their top line revenue but also at the environment they're creating for their employees and the values they want to share with customers."

Emmanuel Nataf, CEO @ reedsy.com

"I found it to be truly fascinating. Every slide that Brett has chosen gives so much insight into the way the company thinks about their culture—and how he has incorporated his thoughts and comments to guide the reader through the handbook"

Laurel Bond, Founder Summit Recruitment

"Great handbook and definitely on top of the pile of books I have read during the past twelve months."

Christian Steyn, Accenture

"Culture Decks Decoded is a must read for anyone serious about creating a scaled and sustainable business. Culture is the ultimate strategic advantage and this handbook gives you the hacks on how to how to learn from the very best culture driven companies"

Peter Ward, Co-founder of WAYN, and Humanity Inc.

"For his new handbook, Bretton Putter taps into his experience both as a consultant to companies about their culture and his experience as a top tier head-hunter to outline how companies like Netflix, Hubspot and Hootsuite use their culture decks to describe their cultures and what makes them unique and different."

Carlos Espinal, Partner Seedcamp

"At last! Someone has created a framework to help founders create a culture deck. This handbook is brilliant in its simplicity."

John Thompson, Chairman, Mentor, Coach & Advisor

"After 38 years of Executive Search for Venture Capital funded startups I have seen my fair share of culture related successes and failures. Brett's planning & design of what culture is required to ensure hiring of the best talent is the best way to win this battle. Reading Culture Decks Decoded is a great first step."

Lee Silver, Founder LA Silver Associates

"17 years of experience working with start-up and high growth companies has allowed Brett to build an elegant and simple framework for the creation of a culture deck."

Paul Archer, CEO Duel

"I really like the concept of this handbook, it's filled with lots of valuable insights. Having come from a company that screamed culture (for nearly 2 decades), I can fully understand why, how, where, and when it's important. And, it's a great reminder for me to continue to work with my team to define our culture. It's made me even more aware of how important a strong culture is during the recruiting and hiring process, when giving feedback on performance and behaviour, as well as the dreaded exercise of firing."

Julie Trell, Global Head (& Chief Human API)

"Culture becomes a defining feature of a company whether it's done intentionally or not. Success or failure can often be traced back to cultural values. It's such an important part of the businesses I have worked in or built that I wish I had read this years ago. With the global digital revolution, never has placing emphasis on your company culture as a definable asset been more important than it is today."

Nora Rothrock, Group Managing Director US Tax and Financial Services Group Limited

TABLE OF CONTENTS

INTRODUCTION

The light bulb moment happened for me a couple of years ago, before I founded CultureGene, the hybrid executive search and company culture consultancy that I now run. When it happened, it felt like I'd been catapulted into a future where leaders make business decisions based on how those decisions support living the values and fulfilling the mission and vision of the company; that future, I sensed, would be realized through Culture-Driven leadership. The leaders who today take a Culture-Driven approach to building their businesses recognize culture as the ultimate asset of their companies… and they treat it as such.

At that point of time in my life, I had spent 14 years as the Managing Partner of an executive search practice, working with early-stage high-growth technology companies in the UK, Europe, and the U.S. Reflecting on the 400+ searches that I had completed during those years, I realized that the most smoothly run searches—those that had the best outcomes—were for CEOs who had a solid understanding of their company's culture.

Achieving an understanding, even at a rudimentary level, of the client company's culture allowed me to source candidates who were not only a suitable match for the required skills and expertise of the role, but—more importantly—as a fit to the culture of the company. This realization—my defining of what the holy grail of candidate sourcing was—resulted in me spending more time in meetings with my clients discussing their company's culture (the values, mission, and vision of the business) than the actual role requirements.

I got hooked on the importance of company culture and decided to set off on a journey to better understand how high-growth companies developed strong and effective cultures. I started to interview CEOs who had invested in building a strong company culture to get to the bottom of exactly when, what, and how they had each gone about developing and leveraging their company culture as a business asset. Perhaps unsurprisingly, I needed to kiss a lot of frogs to find these CEOs; from my research I found that on average, only 10%—1 out of 10!—high-growth companies has bothered to define their company culture. This is an appalling figure, and one that is my duty and mission to help change.

During the research for my forthcoming book *The Culture Gene: Leadership and Culture Development Lessons from High-Growth Companies*, I came across the Netflix Culture Deck, which is the primary inspiration for this handbook. Netflix's CEO Reed Hastings kicked off the online culture deck trend back in 2009 by publicly posting his company's 125-page slide deck online. That culture deck outlines everything from the company's expectations for excellence to its hiring and firing policy, and from why the company pays top dollar packages to what the company values in—and expects from—its employees.

In 2016, Reid Hoffman interviewed Reed Hastings for the Greymatter podcast about what led to the creation of Netflix's famous culture deck; his input is worth noting. Hastings shared how the Netflix situation was about eight years prior to this interview: Netflix had been onboarding new employees, and Hastings himself was feeling frustrated with the process. "I would meet with all the new employees and I would go through this 100-page slide deck. Two out of three [candidates] really got it and understood, and their managers had properly described to them Netflix; one out of three employees were in shock because the deck has some aggressive statements like: 'adequate performance gets a generous severance package' and 'we are a team, not a family'. If you know [that mentality] going in, you can love it; if you don't know it and you didn't expect it, you feel bait-and-switched. So the big driver was that we realized that every candidate should get it—and then if, of course, every candidate is going to get it, then let's just make it public."

When Hoffman asked Hastings if the construction of the culture deck served as central tool for keeping the "cultural norm" as Netflix scaled, Hastings agreed that it did—though perhaps not in the most expected way. "I wouldn't quite say to *keep* a cultural norm," he pointed out, "but one of the keys, was to share and debate. One of the great things about putting things in writing is that it makes it more debatable, so it's not just hearing a sermon […] you can comment and say that *this part here that we wrote down doesn't seem appropriate* or *this part doesn't seem like what we do*."

"To some degree," Hastings added, "[a culture deck] is a bill of rights for employees; here is a set of things that we, the company, want and aspire to operate by, and, if we don't, you can call us out on it and we will either fix the articulation—because it's too easy to misunderstand—or live up to what we want to. So, in some ways, it's aspirational. By putting it in writing […] it allows all the people in the company to collaborate on it and suggest improvements."

Facebook's COO Sheryl Sandberg praised the deck, noting that "it may well be the most important document ever to come out of the Valley." I doubt Hastings imagined that his 125-page document would resonate so strongly with the broader internet community and become such a viral success; as of August 2018, it's garnered over 18 million views on SlideShare.

I also doubt that Hastings would have imagined that his deck would inspire a handbook about how to craft a company culture deck.

WHAT KIND OF CEO ARE YOU, OR WHAT KIND OF CEO DO YOU WORK FOR?

In my 17 years of experience working with high-growth companies, I have found that there are three types of company CEOs.

- The **first** is not interested in wasting his or her time on company culture because it's not that important. In most cases, these CEOs do eventually realize the importance of company culture… but it's often too late.

- The **second** type of CEO believes that company culture is important to the success of his or her business and knows that something must be done about it… but doesn't know where to start.

- The **third** understands, at a fundamental level, that culture is the only competitive advantage that he or she has total control over in the company. Such CEOs therefore take steps to define their company's culture… and actively invest in nurturing and strengthening it to the best of their ability.

Culture Decks Decoded is written for companies led by the latter two types of CEOs. These CEOs understand the critical importance of developing a strong company culture. These CEOs want to build businesses where their people can fulfil their potential and make a difference. These CEOs want to differentiate their company from the competition by communicating and sharing the uniqueness and greatness of their business: the company's definition of what success looks like, how the company deals with failure, what the company looks for and how it attracts the best talent, why you should or shouldn't work there, how the company develops its people, and how they are able to grow, develop themselves and self-actualize.

If you work for the first type of CEO, send him or her a copy of this handbook. You never know. It might just spark a lightbulb moment…

WHAT IS A CULTURE DECK + WHY DO YOU NEED ONE?

As more leaders realize the significant impact that their company culture has across every aspect of their business—and, most significantly, on whether someone decides to work for and ultimately stay with the company for an extended period of time or not—more leaders are creating and openly sharing **culture decks** that help to make their company culture a more visible, tangible, and conscious asset that in turn helps to attract and retain the best talent (and even partners, investors, and clients).

Just as each company's culture is as unique as a fingerprint, culture decks vary greatly in their content, size, style, and description.

- "[Our 125-page deck] was written so that employees could have clarity about what's important for success, what to expect from each other, and to honestly tell the truth about how companies really operate." – Netflix

- "Created by our leadership team with input from people at every level of the company, our culture deck tells the world who we are, what we're about, and what we value." –Acceleration Partners

- "Our employee handbook is a single card that says: 'Use good judgement in all situations.'" – Nordstrom

- "This book isn't about fringe benefits or how to set up your workstation or where to find source code. Valve works in ways that might seem counterintuitive at first. This handbook is about the choices you're going to be making and how to think about them. Mainly, it's about how not to freak out now that you're here." - Valve

- "This document is part manifesto and part employee handbook. It's part who we are and part who we aspire to be." - Hubspot

We all understand that one of the main challenges for leaders who are scaling their company is that of recruiting and hiring the right talent. The company has to not only find the right A+ candidates in an incredibly competitive market, but to also convince them that this company is the right environment for them to succeed, grow, learn, develop, fulfill their potential, and make a difference—especially if the company in question is an underfunded early-stage startup, and one that doesn't have the money to splurge on salaries.

The culture decks that I have chosen for this handbook help companies like Netflix, Valve, Hootsuite, Patreon, Hubspot, and Asana do this in spades.

These documents:

- Inform and reinforce the values, mission and vision of the company.

- Differentiate the company from the competition.

- Encourage potential candidates to self-select in OR self-select out of the recruitment process, before they have wasted anyone's time and resources.

- Attract, recruit, and retain A+ talent.

- Reveal how team members are actively engaged in the company and are able to make a difference and fulfil their potential.

- Outline how processes like onboarding and performance reviews are conducted.

- Demonstrate that there is clarity of purpose, culture, and strategy across the organization.

- Define what the key metrics are, how investments are made, what's rewarded and recognized by the company.

- Describe the importance of hiring for the right values fit, why people are let go, and how promotions are decided upon.

- Describe the learning and development opportunities at the company.

The company culture decks chosen for this handbook are excellent examples of how these companies communicate—in Netflix's case, to over 18 million potential employees!—what they are looking for in prospective employees and why such employees would enjoy working with them.

These culture decks are, in essence, outstanding ambassadors for these respective companies, informing the world about the company's values and its practices. They help answer some of the most fundamental questions that potential employees (and current employees) may have about the business, all while evocatively communicating the character and personality of the company and giving specific readers the insight as to why they should be excited to work there.

CREATING YOUR OWN CULTURE DECK

When researching this handbook and talking to founders, CEOs and Heads of HR/People/Talent about the process of creating their own culture deck, I discovered two critical challenges: first, that there was no overarching document that explained what an effective culture deck consisted of; and, second, that these leaders didn't have enough time to review all of the available decks in order to learn how other such companies had structured and written theirs. Culture Decks Decoded aims to solve these obstructions and to clear the way towards your own formulation of a unique and powerful culture deck.

You must always remember, when crafting yours, that your company culture is as unique as a strand of your DNA: similar in some ways to other people's, perhaps, but ultimately inimitable. In designing your culture deck, you should create the structure, design, and content that works for your specific culture and organization. As always, however, borrowing from what others have successfully done before will enable you to avoid re-inventing the wheel. Many companies have created tremendous culture decks that effectively communicate their culture to potential and current employees, customers, investors, and partners. You can certainly receive inspiration from their content and from the way in which they've created and structured such meaningful culture decks.

The culture decks of the companies I have chosen—Netflix, Hubspot, Valve, LinkedIn, Hootsuite and Asana among others—are unique (granted, some do borrow from Netflix's deck; frankly it's so good and effective, I'm not surprised). Netflix's deck is sparse, Hubspot and Hootsuite's decks are nicely designed, LinkedIn uses a lot of people and team photographs, and Valve uses a lot of text. Please note, too, that the culture decks I have chosen are not structured in the way that I've laid them out in this handbook; I have chosen slides that I believe get the message across to the reader effectively, and have organized them into the structure described below for ease of study and review only.

- The company **CULTURE**.

- The company's **MISSION**.

- The company's **VISION**.

- The company's **HISTORY**.

- The **VALUES** and how the company lives those values.

- What's most **UNIQUE** or special about the way the company does what it does.

- How **ONBOARDING** works.

- How the company approaches **DIVERSITY AND INCLUSION**.

- How the company deals with **FAILURE**.

- How the company fosters **TRANSPARENCY**.

- What employee **PERKS AND BENEFITS** the company offers.

- How the company creates a workplace where **PEOPLE** can make a difference, fulfil their potential and self-actualize.

- How the company attracts and **RETAINS A+ TALENT**.

- What it means to be a member of the team and work **ENVIRONMENT**.

Where relevant, I have also provided my opinion on the content of the slide (or group of slides) and on how that content resonates with me, or how it may resonate with someone who might be interested in working at the company.

Within this handbook, *Culture Decks Decoded*, my hope is that you will begin to understand—or further solidify your conviction in—the necessity of defining and investing in your culture, as well as with what tremendous advantages a Culture-Driven strategy will provide you. Culture is something that must be manifested and embodied daily through behaviors that align with core values; crafting a straightforward and thoughtful culture deck will allow you to attract like-minded candidates and reinforce the behaviors you expect from your team while broadcasting your unique culture to a global audience. Treat your culture deck as a window into your own company's operating system, for it is indeed the account of your company's character, personality, behaviors, practices, and norms, as well as the outline of its purpose for having a place in society. Remember that the company's culture evolves as the company progresses, the "way we work around here" is different when the team is 10, to when the team is 50 or a 100 strong. It's important to ensure that your company culture deck is iterated upon and kept up to date.

I hope that you enjoy reading through the following material and find it valuable as you develop your own company's distinctive culture deck.

HOW TO USE THIS HANDBOOK:

1. Review the slide or group of slides.
2. Read the copy and decide if you resonate with the text and tone of the slide or not. Explore further why you do or don't. Place yourself in a potential employee's shoes – imagine how they would feel reading it.
3. If the slide contains an image ask yourself how relevant that image is, what you feel about it and what, if anything, the image tells you about the company.
4. Compare with my thoughts about the slide.
5. There are no right or wrong perspectives, so take notes for your future deck on what works for you and what doesn't.

NOTES:

eShares has rebranded to Carta.com

Hotjar does not currently have a culture deck, but they do have a team manual, which I explore in more detail in this handbook. If you haven't yet gotten around to developing your culture deck, the Hotjar team manual is a great example of an alternative first step towards getting the company's culture across to potential employees and the team.

Next Jump, recognized as a Deliberately Developmental Organization, does not have a culture deck but the company does run culture tours for executives of companies who wish to understand how Next Jump operates. Next Jump have shared their culture tour slides with me and I have selected relevant slides for further exploration in this handbook.

CULTURE

Culture develops from day one of a business and becomes embedded when decisions that are made prove to be successful, and the thinking that went into those decisions becomes "the way we do things around here". Culture happens, and it will *always* generate visible results. The choice lies in if and how the leaders choose to cultivate that culture. The companies in this chapter understand how important their culture is and use culture-focused slides to set the tone of the deck. The culture section specifically defines what culture means to the company, how the company perceive its ongoing importance and its contribution to their business's sustainable success. In some cases, for clarity the company explicitly states what culture *isn't*. In this chapter we have slides from LinkedIn, POSSIBLE, Netflix, Nanoheal, Hubspot, Morey Creative Studios, Nanigans, Soundstripe, Hootsuite, Nordstrom, Hostinger, Patreon and Next Jump.

LINKEDIN

IT'S WHO WE ARE

——— AND ———

WHO WE ASPIRE TO BE

IT'S OUR

CULTURE

THAT HAS ENABLED LINKEDIN
TO GET WHERE IT IS TODAY

EVERY ONE OF US
STRIVES TO UPHOLD OUR

CULTURE
— AND —
VALUES

AND WE BELIEVE IT'S OUR

CULTURE

THAT WILL ENABLE LINKEDIN TO
ACHIEVE ITS VISION AND MISSION

CULTURE

MISSION

VISION

HISTORY

VALUES

THE WAY
WE WORK
AROUND HERE

ONBOARDING

DIVERSITY
+
INCLUSION

FAILURE

TALENT

TRANSPARENCY

FEEDBACK

EMPLOYEE
BENEFITS

MAKE A
DIFFERENCE

BONUS

LinkedIn uses four slides in their deck to demonstrate how important the culture has been to the health, unity, and identity of the company; its leaders clearly recognise its ongoing importance. These slides give a feeling of welcoming, vitality, creativity, and camaraderie. I like the wording on the first and third slides, specifically using the word "enables" rather than something like "that will enable"; indicating that LinkedIn has already solidified a healthy culture. The culture strikes me immediately as young and I get a sense from the fourth slide that there's a "work hard, play hard" vibe in the company. The character of the company comes across as fun, unified, social, playful, expressive, and cool.

POSSIBLE

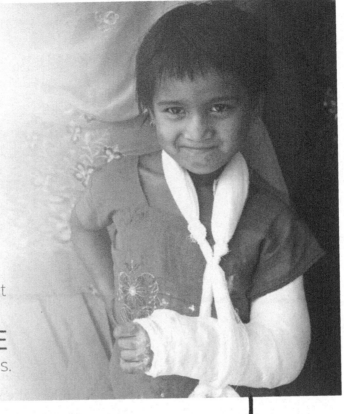

The driving force
behind our for-impact
culture is to get
REMARKABLE
results for our patients.

CULTURE

↓

MISSION

↓

VISION

↓

HISTORY

↓

VALUES

↓

THE WAY
WE WORK
AROUND HERE

↓

ONBOARDING

↓

DIVERSITY
+
INCLUSION

↓

FAILURE

↓

TALENT

↓

TRANSPARENCY

↓

FEEDBACK

↓

EMPLOYEE
BENEFITS

↓

MAKE A
DIFFERENCE

↓

BONUS

POSSIBLE's first culture definition slide is evocative and informative. The slide instantly exudes the sense that this is a purpose-driven organization. The slide talks about the "driving force", a "for-impact culture", and "remarkable results", phrases which demonstrate that this organization means business. The child in the image sports a broken arm yet is also wearing a heartfelt (albeit shy) and almost sassy smile and a clean white cast; this backs up the slide's promise of *remarkable* results. It is a photo that speaks of hope and aid, and one that I think ties in well to the company culture of purpose-driven, "for-impact" actions.

Great teams bring the same entrepreneurial energy to improving their culture as they do to improving their product.

Minimal and brief, this slide informs the reader about how teams are expected to apply the same entrepreneurial energy—not just to living, but also *improving* POSSIBLE's culture. Very few companies go so far as to connect the act of improving the company culture to improving the product, thereby highlighting how important this alignment is to the company; it also makes the culture more tangible to the reader.

ACCELERATION PARTNERS

OUR CULTURE & TEAM

We are proud to have built a world-class company culture that we believe gives us a competitive advantage. Our employees are team players, intellectually curious, resilient, innovative, strategic and results-driven. And people have noticed! We have been recognized as a best workplace for Women, Flexibility and Advertising & Marketing by Great Place to Work® and Fortune. And we were named to Ad Age's Best Places to Work list.

We are true to our core values and enable our employees to engage in challenging and rewarding work while achieving personal and professional goals. We believe that engaged, happy employees, both at work and in their personal lives, are the foundation of a successful and sustainable growth business.

Our team members live our core values each and every day; love what they do and who they do it with; and work with an energy and passion that is contagious. AP-ers are excited to work with other motivated and talented teammates and stretch their limits.

We define A-players on our team as people who live our core values, are in the "right seat" at the right time, enjoy doing what they do and are the best at it. We all appreciate that if someone is not a value fit or cannot find the right seat, we must act respectfully to help the employee find a better opportunity elsewhere.

We offer significant flexibility and the ability to work from home for all employees and we have core geographic hubs in Boston, New York, Philadelphia, Chicago, Denver, and Southern California which provide us the opportunity to collaborate and socialize locally with colleagues.

CULTURE

MISSION

VISION

HISTORY

VALUES

THE WAY
WE WORK
AROUND HERE

ONBOARDING

DIVERSITY
+
INCLUSION

FAILURE

TALENT

TRANSPARENCY

FEEDBACK

EMPLOYEE
BENEFITS

MAKE A
DIFFERENCE

BONUS

Annually we host the AP Summit and bring all of our team members together for a week of learning, socializing and teambuilding activities that has become a cornerstone of our culture. Everyone looks forward to this annual event and shares stories about their favorite activity or speaker from a past year. New employees are eager to attend and meet the entire company for the first time.

Service and giving back to our local communities is important to everyone at Acceleration Partners. Team members regularly organize volunteer days in their local communities and we are generous with our knowledge, resources and time for causes that our employees are passionate about. We love seeing pictures of our teams volunteering locally and using their volunteer PTO for causes that are meaningful to them.

Acceleration Partners is a sought-after thought leader on topics related to performance marketing and company culture, leadership and growth. Our team is regularly asked to speak and contribute on these topics and we love to spread the wealth.

I really like this slide from Acceleration Partners, which pretty much covers all the bases. The sceptical person may think that this is all marketing speak however the company demonstrates that it walks the talk by proudly showing the many awards it has won for its workplace culture.

In this slide the company:

- Recognises culture as competitive advantage.

- Hires team players who are intellectually curious, resilient, innovative, strategic and results driven.

- Has created an environment where their people can fulfil their potential.

- Employs people who live the core values daily and are passionate about what they do.

- Understands that not everyone will fit in with their company and if someone doesn't fit they will help them find a better suited opportunity elsewhere.

- Offers workplace flexibility.

- Hosts a week-long learning and teambuilding summit.

- Gives back to the local community.

NETFLIX

Netflix Culture:
Freedom & Responsibility

We Seek Excellence

Our culture focuses on helping us achieve excellence

Netflix's first slide communicates that it has two core values; freedom and responsibility, which work together to create a whole (as such, they are both mutually co-dependent and mandatory). The feel of this slide is minimalistic and influenced by eastern philosophies (the yin-yang symbolism here is simple yet effective). The second slide sets the cultural standards for the organization: to seek excellence; the role of the company's culture in achieving that is clearly stated. Overall, Netflix's design is direct and straightforward.

CULTURE

MISSION

VISION

HISTORY

VALUES

THE WAY WE WORK AROUND HERE

ONBOARDING

DIVERSITY + INCLUSION

FAILURE

TALENT

TRANSPARENCY

FEEDBACK

EMPLOYEE BENEFITS

MAKE A DIFFERENCE

BONUS

HOTJAR

Welcome to the Hotjar Team Manual

In this manual you will get an overview of our company vision and core values, what it's like to work here, how we work together as a unified team (even though we all work remotely), how we recruit new team mates, and some practical information about being a Hotjar team member.

This manual is separated into two sections which each have corresponding pages. Please explore and enjoy!

> About Hotjar
> Working at Hotjar

IMPORTANT: Please note that some links inside this manual will not work for people who are not Hotjar Team Members.

Want to know even more about Hotjar? Have a look through the links below:

- Hotjar - our product and Product Updates
- Outside the Jar - our Hotjar blog, including posts about behind the scenes at Hotjar, working as a remote company, finding success as a start-up
- The Humans Strike Back - our weekly podcast interviewing individuals and companies who have earned their wins by putting people first
- Hotjar Weekly Webinars - live webinars with a member of our team to help learn how best to use and get the most out of our product
- Apply to work at Hotjar - visit our careers page to see our current openings

The opening page of Hotjar's team manual is really appealing, telling me quite a bit about the culture at Hotjar. Firstly, they've thought and care enough about culture and the team to create a detailed team manual that covers everything from the vision and core values to the company podcasts. Secondly, that they've created it both for internal and external use, with only the inner circle being able to access certain links. Third, even though they're a fully-remote team, they clearly invest the time and money to get together and bond as a team — in the above case, to go skiing/snowboarding, which looks like a lot of fun. The links below the picture reveal more about the culture. This organization clearly enjoys playing with language and has a good sense of humour, in fact I immediately subscribed to the podcast.

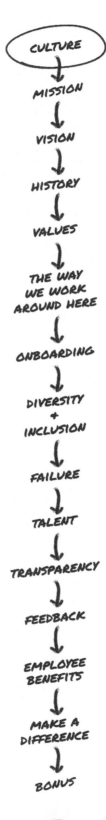

NANOHEAL

Culture is what happens when the boss is not around.

This slide does a great job on its own of communicating to the reader what culture means at Nanoheal. The wording makes the reader pause and think and the image is minimal yet powerful. The phrase "culture is what happens when the boss is not around" really hits the nail on the head: the core issue is that, to really see a culture in action, you need to see how people work, behave, and treat each other when they aren't being supervised.

Nanoheal adds a second slide to go into more detail about exactly what the company means by "culture". The company comes across as forward-thinking and both of these slides indicate that culture has been thought about in some depth. The slides are bright and visually engaging and they carry a clear, strong message about how Nanoheal feels regarding culture. The symbols that are used do help to enhance the overall message. The continuity between the slides is excellent. Considering this second slide, I might paraphrase the four core values of Nanoheal as **ALIGNMENT, MASTERY, PURPOSE,** and **INTEGRITY**.

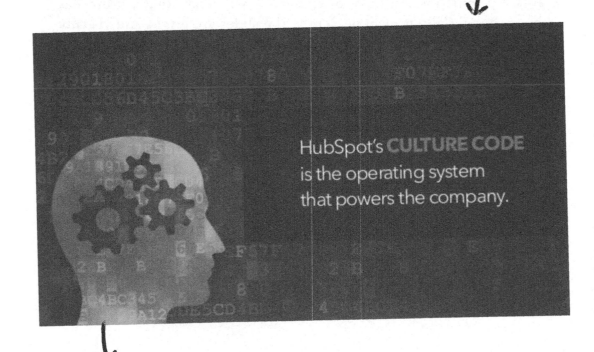

WHAT'S CULTURE?
A set of shared beliefs, values and practices.

HubSpot's **CULTURE CODE** is the operating system that powers the company.

WHY DO WE ~~CARE ABOUT~~ OBSESS OVER CULTURE?

Culture doesn't just help **attract** amazing people, it **amplifies** their abilities and helps them do their best work.

CULTURE

MISSION

VISION

HISTORY

VALUES

THE WAY WE WORK AROUND HERE

ONBOARDING

DIVERSITY + INCLUSION

FAILURE

TALENT

TRANSPARENCY

FEEDBACK

EMPLOYEE BENEFITS

MAKE A DIFFERENCE

BONUS

BRETTON PUTTER

CULTURE HAPPENS.

Whether planned or not,
all companies have a culture.

So why not create a **culture we love**?

The Hubspot slides immediately communicate authority, intelligence, and depth of thought about culture, most likely reflecting the character of the company. The definition of culture as "a set of shared beliefs, values, and practices" communicates that this company has thought about what culture is and why it's relevant and important. The second slide cleverly correlates culture to the company's operating system; if I were a potential employee, I'd take special note of—and appreciate—the emphasis on the company's *obsession* over culture with the use of the strikethrough on the third slide.

These slides make me think that there is a level of attention to culture in this company that other companies strive for years to attain. The fourth and fifth slides in the Hubspot deck make the company even more appealing; they're visually attractive and the words jump off the page. The use of different sized fonts and a mix of capitalized and lower-case lettering keeps my interest. The language used ("attract amazing people" and "amplifies their abilities") is likewise appealing (it also makes me wonder if the assonance was deliberate).

The acknowledgement on the fifth slide that "culture happens" (playing with the well-known phrase: "shit happens") is again humorous and straightforward, and the slide allows a new hire to understand that the company is deliberate in its efforts to create a strong culture.

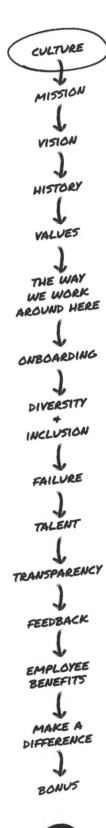

MOREY CREATIVE STUDIOS

Culture Happens

Culture happens whether it is identified or not.

Ours grew out of a founding group of the right people.
We have documented it here to ensure we grow with the same caliber of people.

In this slide, Morey Creative Studios alerts the reader to the fact that culture is innate and happens anyway, "whether it is identified or not". This phrase creates tension in the reader's mind; fairly enough, the sentences that follow remove the tension by explaining where the Morey culture came from and how the company has documented the culture to ensure that the company hires the right calibre of people. This is clever, as they are indicating that culture is perpetual and must constantly be cultivated and nurtured. The images are quite engaging; the dog, doughnuts, and team photos show a culture that blends work (especially collaborative work) with enjoyment.

It's also interesting to see that Morey uses the exact same phrase as Hubspot—*Culture Happens*—and have an image of someone wearing a Hubspot T-shirt on the first page. I wonder what, if any, connection there might be between the two companies.

We Are All Vectors

vec·tor
/ˈvektər/ noun

In mathematics or physics, a vector is a quantity having direction as well as magnitude, especially as determining the position of one point in space relative to another.

CULTURE
↓
MISSION
↓
VISION
↓
HISTORY
↓
VALUES
↓
THE WAY WE WORK AROUND HERE
↓
ONBOARDING
↓
DIVERSITY + INCLUSION
↓
FAILURE
↓
TALENT
↓
TRANSPARENCY
↓
FEEDBACK
↓
EMPLOYEE BENEFITS
↓
MAKE A DIFFERENCE
↓
BONUS

We Are All Vectors

If we are all vectors moving forward but in different directions, we are not as effectively moving the company forward.

We Are All Vectors

This Culture Code is intended to keep us all moving in the right direction.

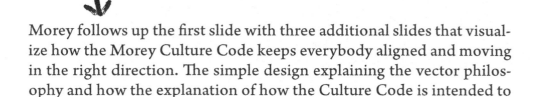

Morey follows up the first slide with three additional slides that visualize how the Morey Culture Code keeps everybody aligned and moving in the right direction. The simple design explaining the vector philosophy and how the explanation of how the Culture Code is intended to keep everyone in the company moving in the right direction is effective, visually appealing and clever.

NANIGANS

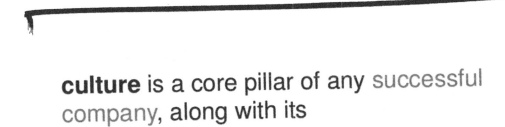

"94% of executives and 88% of employees believe a **distinct workplace culture** is important to business success."

- Deloitte, "Culture in the Workplace" study

culture is a core pillar of any successful company, along with its

- industry
- product
- customers

Nanigans uses these slides and the external statistics to highlight how significant company culture is to business success. By highlighting the Deloitte study, the Nanigans team is subtly showing the reader that the company is actually delivering on what the majority of executives believe to be true for business success.

and yet for 3 years at **nanigans**, we didn't really talk about "our culture."

nanigans

CULTURE

↓

MISSION

↓

VISION

↓

HISTORY

↓

VALUES

↓

THE WAY
WE WORK
AROUND HERE

↓

ONBOARDING

↓

DIVERSITY
+
INCLUSION

↓

FAILURE

↓

TALENT

↓

TRANSPARENCY

↓

FEEDBACK

↓

EMPLOYEE
BENEFITS

↓

MAKE A
DIFFERENCE

↓

BONUS

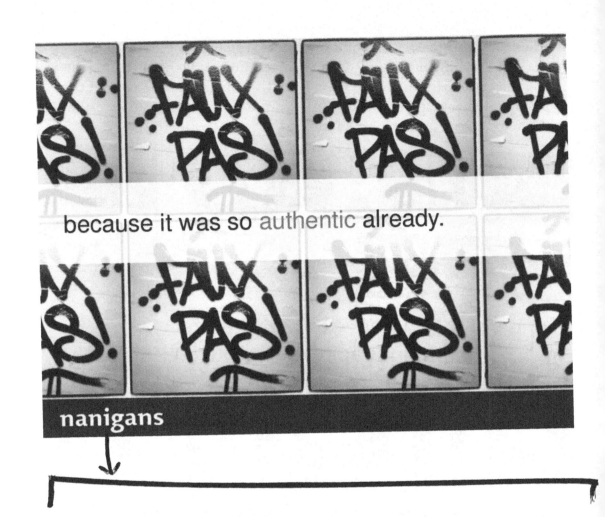

because it was so authentic already.

nanigans

genuine culture is organic, not imposed.

it emanates from people,
a natural expression of who they are,
and arises out of shared experiences.

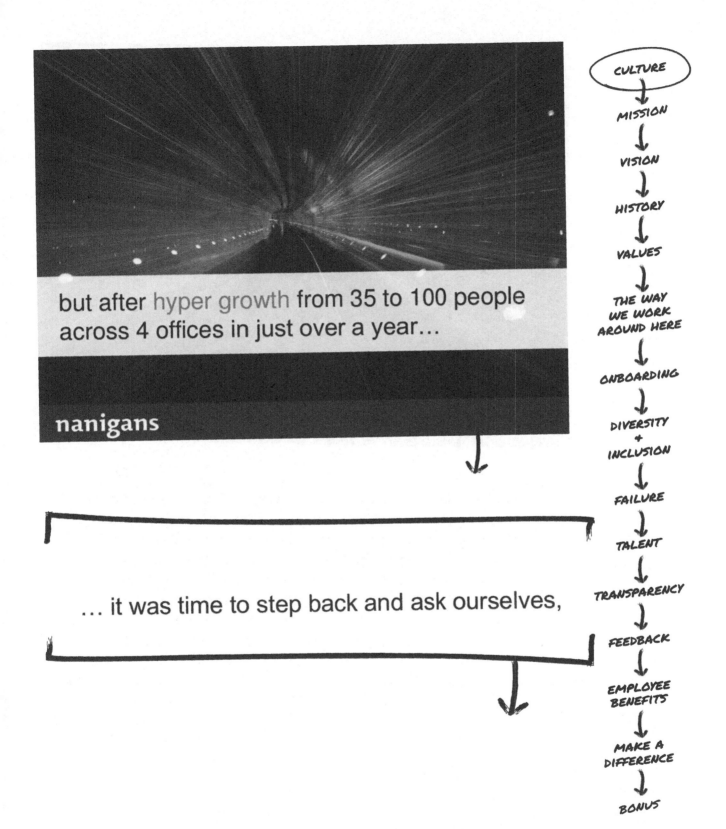

but after hyper growth from 35 to 100 people across 4 offices in just over a year…

nanigans

… it was time to step back and ask ourselves,

CULTURE

MISSION

VISION

HISTORY

VALUES

THE WAY
WE WORK
AROUND HERE

ONBOARDING

DIVERSITY
+
INCLUSION

FAILURE

TALENT

TRANSPARENCY

FEEDBACK

EMPLOYEE
BENEFITS

MAKE A
DIFFERENCE

BONUS

WHAT DEFINES A GREAT COMPANY?

nanigans

The rest of the Nanigans slides (with very different design styles) tell the story of how the company came to address its culture, which (like most high-growth companies) they didn't really discuss during the initial stages of their growth. They finally recognized culture's intrinsic importance after the company had experienced a twelve-month period of rapid growth and (I would assume!) some of the growing pains associated with doubling the size of the team and opening new offices. The Nanigans team was fortunate enough (in my experience not all startups are) to have built a strong (yet undefined) culture during the first three years of business. They were smart to quickly realize how important defining a culture becomes when a company scales.

SOUNDSTRIPE

Culture is NOT:

Daycare
Espresso
Health benefits
Sushi lunches
Game rooms
etc.

Our culture is the values and standards we work and live by. Yes, we do have a pingpong table *(typical)* and strive to have a "cool" office but those things do not define our culture. Our people do.

CULTURE

↓

MISSION

↓

VISION

↓

HISTORY

↓

VALUES

↓

THE WAY
WE WORK
AROUND HERE

↓

ONBOARDING

↓

DIVERSITY
+
INCLUSION

↓

FAILURE

↓

TALENT

↓

TRANSPARENCY

↓

FEEDBACK

↓

EMPLOYEE
BENEFITS

↓

MAKE A
DIFFERENCE

↓

BONUS

These Soundstripe slides describing the company culture are unpretentious yet potent. They take a different approach, cutting to the core of a common misunderstanding about culture; you don't create culture with perks, benefits, or gimmicks. The slides emphasise that culture is actually about the company's values and standards that the people live and work by—and that you still can, of course, certainly have the "cool" office as part of that. The language of the slide is playfully self-deprecatory ("yes, we do have a ping-pong table (*typical*)"), but this feels very deliberate. The focus is on making the point that culture is fundamentally about one thing: people.

HOOTSUITE

This document is a resource for all Hootsuite employees. We give this to each new team member who joins us.

Hootsuite's Manifesto contains our core principles, some stories of our history and culture, and a special Peepsbook.

Introduction · Purpose

🦉 Hootsuite

CULTURE

↓

MISSION

↓

VISION

↓

HISTORY

↓

VALUES

↓

THE WAY
WE WORK
AROUND HERE

↓

ONBOARDING

↓

DIVERSITY
+
INCLUSION

↓

FAILURE

↓

TALENT

↓

TRANSPARENCY

↓

FEEDBACK

↓

EMPLOYEE
BENEFITS

↓

MAKE A
DIFFERENCE

↓

BONUS

Our Culture

A passionate, egoless team having fun
building something bigger than itself.

Indeed, like other great companies
before us, we discovered that
culture is the gravity of a successful,
fast-growing company.

It's the constant, steady force that
binds us together and keeps us
focused and driven.

**It's what makes people want
to come to work every day.**
It's what makes us stronger than
our competitors.

Our Culture

This manifesto makes sure we hit the brakes and take a snapshot of the most important aspects of Hootsuite's culture today.

"FOR THE PEEPLE* BY THE PEEPLE."

This manifesto was created as a bottoms-up document. Employees from across the organization were asked to provide input on what they feel.

* (At Hootsuite, we sometimes like to call each other peeps when talking about large groups.)

"Peeps" and "Peeple" is a social media twist on "People", and I like the fact that the Hootsuite team have adopted such terms into their own language at the company, which is a common practice amongst the companies that are able to develop cult-like company cultures. It feels familial and inclusive. "For the people..." is also a great mantra to have, it carries weight and is easily remembered since it echoes the words in Abraham Lincoln's Gettysburg Address, as well as many other political documents throughout the world.

CULTURE
↓
MISSION
↓
VISION
↓
HISTORY
↓
VALUES
↓
THE WAY WE WORK AROUND HERE
↓
ONBOARDING
↓
DIVERSITY + INCLUSION
↓
FAILURE
↓
TALENT
↓
TRANSPARENCY
↓
FEEDBACK
↓
EMPLOYEE BENEFITS
↓
MAKE A DIFFERENCE
↓
BONUS

"Here there's an overall sense of curiosity and inquisitiveness. It seems everyone is always chipping away at something everyone is trying to push something somewhere. It's a culture of optimism."

Josh Lamb
Software Engineer
(formerly Junior Accountant)

The Hootsuite slides put a smile on my face and do a great job of explaining what the manifesto consists of and what it is for. They explain the culture, which is about being egoless, humble, "building something bigger than itself", and having fun. I particularly like the way that the company uses gravity in the third of this selection of slides to describe its culture as something that is constant, ever-present, yet invisible (apart from the effect it has). The company describes one of the outcomes of the culture as a place where "people want to come to work" and highlights that its culture is what differentiates Hootsuite from the competition.

The company has a young, vibrant, energetic feel, which is supported again by the images and the words used: as Josh on the final slide is quoted as saying, there is "an overall sense of inquisitiveness" and "a culture of optimism"—this doesn't feel forced and it does have the desired effect of making the company attractive and the document relatable for a potential employee or new hire. My impression of these slides is that they are highly effective at communicating a quick yet quite telling degree of insight into the culture of the company.

CULTURE
↓
MISSION
↓
VISION
↓
HISTORY
↓
VALUES
↓
THE WAY
WE WORK
AROUND HERE
↓
ONBOARDING
↓
DIVERSITY
+
INCLUSION
↓
FAILURE
↓
TALENT
↓
TRANSPARENCY
↓
FEEDBACK
↓
EMPLOYEE
BENEFITS
↓
MAKE A
DIFFERENCE
↓
BONUS

NORDSTROM

Why focus on culture?

For <u>114</u> years, Nordstrom culture has been passed down as new employees join our company.

In a changing world, we'll never forget our heritage of the shoe salesperson, on one knee, assisting one customer at a time.

This slide by Nordstrom conjures up a brilliant image that is extremely effective and highly relevant: the icon of personalized, humble, individual, devoted service, as personified by a dedicated shoe salesperson.

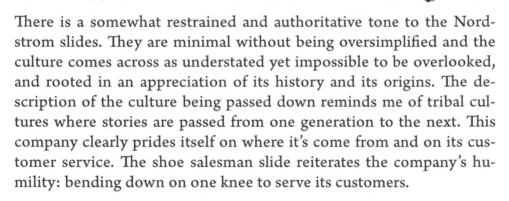

Our #1 priority is **always** the customer!

What makes outstanding customer experiences?

TOP EMPLOYEES.

What makes top employees engaged?

GREAT CULTURE!

CULTURE

MISSION

VISION

HISTORY

VALUES

THE WAY
WE WORK
AROUND HERE

ONBOARDING

DIVERSITY
+
INCLUSION

FAILURE

TALENT

TRANSPARENCY

FEEDBACK

EMPLOYEE
BENEFITS

MAKE A
DIFFERENCE

BONUS

There is a somewhat restrained and authoritative tone to the Nordstrom slides. They are minimal without being oversimplified and the culture comes across as understated yet impossible to be overlooked, and rooted in an appreciation of its history and its origins. The description of the culture being passed down reminds me of tribal cultures where stories are passed from one generation to the next. This company clearly prides itself on where it's come from and on its customer service. The shoe salesman slide reiterates the company's humility: bending down on one knee to serve its customers.

I like the circular causality of the last slide: that outstanding customer experiences will be created by top employees, top employees will be engaged to create outstanding customer experiences by a great culture, and that in turn a great culture will attract top employees. There's also the side note and reminder up in the corner—that the customer is always the company's top priority—and I like the wording of that. It's different (and arguably more truthful) than saying that the customer comes first or is always right.

HOSTINGER

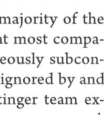

Company Culture is the way we really get
things done. It's what people outside of
the company **feel about the company**

but **don't see.**

HOSTINGER

Hostinger uses a brilliant metaphor here. Just as the majority of the iceberg was mostly invisible to the Titanic, so it is that most companies have a culture that is omnipresent, but simultaneously subconscious and intangible, lurking beneath the surface and ignored by and invisible to the majority (if not everyone). The Hostinger team explains to the reader that culture is the way that their company *really* gets things done, and links the culture to how customers and other external associates feel about the company, even though they don't recognise these reactions as stemming from the culture of the company.

PATREON

What is culture?

Culture is a group of people repeating behaviors.

When people say they like our culture, they're saying they like the way we treat
each other, our visitors, our creators, and our patrons.

Similar (though less striking) to Hostinger's culture slide of the iceberg, Patreon's culture slide is effective in explaining that culture—vastly intangible itself, yet with very tangible results—develops through the perpetual process of a group of people learning about what behaviors result in success and repeating those behaviors, both within and beyond the company.

CULTURE
↓
MISSION
↓
VISION
↓
HISTORY
↓
VALUES
↓
THE WAY
WE WORK
AROUND HERE
↓
ONBOARDING
↓
DIVERSITY
+
INCLUSION
↓
FAILURE
↓
TALENT
↓
TRANSPARENCY
↓
FEEDBACK
↓
EMPLOYEE
BENEFITS
↓
MAKE A
DIFFERENCE
↓
BONUS

NEXT JUMP

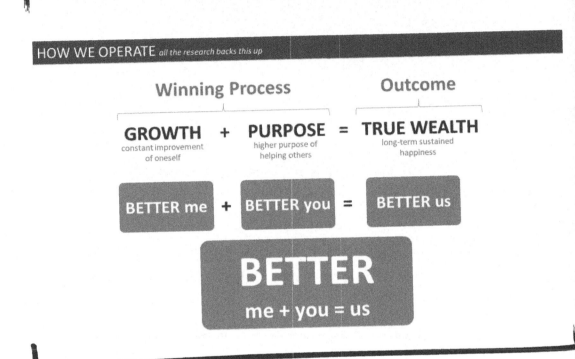

HOW WE OPERATE *all the research backs this up*

Winning Process   **Outcome**

GROWTH + **PURPOSE** = **TRUE WEALTH**
constant improvement   higher purpose of   long-term sustained
of oneself   helping others   happiness

BETTER me + BETTER you = BETTER us

BETTER
me + you = us

As far as company culture goes, Next Jump is the future. I know this is a bold statement but I have had the pleasure of getting to know the London team over the past year and am blown away (literally every time I meet them) by the progress that they are making at the cutting edge of company culture development. The easiest way to demonstrate how far ahead Next Jump is on the culture development journey is to use a 1-10 scale; if a regular start-up is a 1, and Netflix is a 5, then Next Jump is an 8 (no company will ever hit 10; there's always room for improvement and the sky is the limit).

Next Jump's culture is perfectly described by the slide above: Better Me + Better You = Better Us. The slide is visually clear and the formula is intuitive; it seems familiar and totally logical at the same time. It's also really easy to remember. I like the way they have added an extra layer of detail onto this slide to highlight that growth and purpose create the "winning process" that leads to the outcome of "true wealth." It's instantly clear that this is a company that isn't just out to make a profit. The wellbeing and fulfilment of its employees, partners, and community seem to be central to its purpose and focus, and the slide demonstrates a sophisticated understanding that actually creating a "better us" is exactly what will ultimately elevate the performance within the company and the broader ecosystem. The results can't help but be marvelous.

CULTURE
↓
MISSION
↓
VISION
↓
HISTORY
↓
VALUES
↓
THE WAY WE WORK AROUND HERE
↓
ONBOARDING
↓
DIVERSITY + INCLUSION
↓
FAILURE
↓
TALENT
↓
TRANSPARENCY
↓
FEEDBACK
↓
EMPLOYEE BENEFITS
↓
MAKE A DIFFERENCE
↓
BONUS

The mission describes the organization's visible, tangible work in the world: what the company does, who it does it for, and how this helps the client. It explains the tangible activities and overall approach that the company should take as it translates the big picture vision into everyday action. Some companies are solely mission-driven, while other companies have a mission fused with a vision. In this chapter we have slides from Soundstripe, Patreon, GoDaddy, Etsy ROI Online, and Hootsuite.

SOUNDSTRIPE

Our mission is to keep creatives creating.

We are here to serve. Each of our core values are designed around this one very simple mission:

To keep creatives, creating.

This Soundstripe slide is spectacular—it's so simple yet very clever. The mission is focused, clear, and memorable. From this slide in particular, I get the following impressions: creative people work at the company; the company understands what makes creative people tick and realizes what gets in the way of creativity being unleashed; and that serving creative people is at the very heart of what matters at Soundstripe. The company also uses this slide to connect the mission with the core values.

The mission is also generalized enough to encompass as many industries as necessary—"creatives" can be filmmakers, writers, sculptors, graphic designers, and so on—yet, despite the size of the company's target market, the mission statement doesn't feel vague or thoughtless.

GODADDY

OUR MISSION

WE ARE HERE TO HELP OUR CUSTOMERS KICK ASS. WE DO THAT BY LIVING OUR STRATEGY AND RUTHLESSLY PRIORITIZING OUR WORK TO CREATE SIMPLE, ELEGANT TECHNOLOGY THAT DELIGHTS OUR CUSTOMERS—ALL WHILE DELIVERING SERVICE THAT IS SECOND TO NONE. EVERY SINGLE DAY, WE JOIN FORCES ACROSS TEAMS AND GROUPS TO BREAK DOWN BARRIERS, BUILD NEW MARKETS AND STARE DOWN THE IMPOSSIBLE UNTIL THE IMPOSSIBLE BLINKS.

The voice of this GoDaddy slide is fresh, bold, playful, and ambitious, which I imagine reflects the culture within the company. Even though there are a lot of words on this slide, and even though it's in all caps (which generally isn't advisable for large chunks of text), I somehow enjoyed reading this slide. The mission feels clear and very well-articulated. The descriptors used—*elegant, simple, ruthlessly prioritising, second to none, delight, break down barriers*—paint a clear picture of the level of service that the company aims to deliver.

My favorite phrases are the unexpected "help our customers kick ass" at the beginning and the closing statement of "stare down the impossible until the impossible blinks." I sense a real passion in this company, which is visually mirrored in the use of capital letters, the woman's clothing, and the "heat" of the kitchen setting. Overall, to me this slide communicates a professional and ambitious culture where the company understands how to prioritize, is customer focused, delivers a great service, and promotes teamwork.

CULTURE

MISSION

VISION

HISTORY

VALUES

THE WAY
WE WORK
AROUND HERE

ONBOARDING

DIVERSITY
+
INCLUSION

FAILURE

TALENT

TRANSPARENCY

FEEDBACK

EMPLOYEE
BENEFITS

MAKE A
DIFFERENCE

BONUS

ETSY

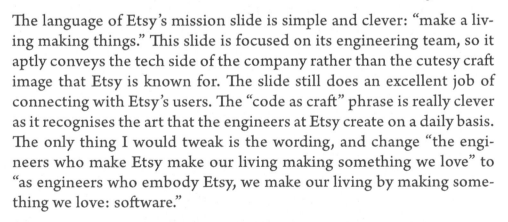

"At Etsy, our mission is to enable people to make a living making things. The engineers who make Etsy make our living making something we love: software. We think of our code as craft."

The language of Etsy's mission slide is simple and clever: "make a living making things." This slide is focused on its engineering team, so it aptly conveys the tech side of the company rather than the cutesy craft image that Etsy is known for. The slide still does an excellent job of connecting with Etsy's users. The "code as craft" phrase is really clever as it recognises the art that the engineers at Etsy create on a daily basis. The only thing I would tweak is the wording, and change "the engineers who make Etsy make our living making something we love" to "as engineers who embody Etsy, we make our living by making something we love: software."

In the sense of context, I think this slide also does an outstanding job because it bridges the gap between creatives/makers and engineers, who may share very similar qualities (passion, innovation, creativity, etc.); the company performs some brilliant positioning here in describing its engineers as "crafters" in a target market of crafters.

ROI ONLINE

What Is ROI Online's Mission?

We help businesses succeed by shaping their marketing and influencing their culture.

The copy of ROI Online's mission is straightforward and pragmatic. The mission is clear: it's a photograph with many symbols and implications, and is powerful without being overwhelming. This image is cute; it's also clever and eye-catching. "ROI" (Return on Investment) implies a future activity, which is further implied by the image of a child, who can also be interpreted as representing "the future"—and if they are kickass as a kid, imagine how unstoppable they'll be as a grown adult! The boxer's glove implies that this company is unstoppable, has great might and influence, powers through all obstacles, and won't give up without a fight; the mask and cape imply super "powers", optimism, a mission to help others and stand up for justice, and so forth.

HOOTSUITE

Mission

Our mission is to empower organizations to turn messages into meaningful relationships.

The Hootsuite mission is clear and compelling. In a world full of social media, where businesses are striving to create meaningful relationships with their community, the Hootsuite people demonstrate that they understand the power of these relationships and how to foster them.

CULTURE

MISSION

VISION

HISTORY

VALUES

THE WAY
WE WORK
AROUND HERE

ONBOARDING

DIVERSITY
+
INCLUSION

FAILURE

TALENT

TRANSPARENCY

FEEDBACK

EMPLOYEE
BENEFITS

MAKE A
DIFFERENCE

BONUS

PATREON

We Have Two Missions

1. Fund the emerging creative class
2. Create a company where teammates build fulfilling lives

Patreon could have written these two mission statements as one; however, they chose to keep them separate. This sparks my curiosity and intrigues me to want to discover more about what to me appears to be this company's balanced set of priorities. The first mission is outwardly focused on the client/beneficiary: the "creative class", which in itself is a strong term that carries additional meaning; the second statement is internally focused on the company. This is very effective; even without using the word "culture", it's crystal clear that culture matters at Patreon. The use of the word "teammate" communicates something about how people are perceived by the senior leadership in the company—everyone is a teammate; there is respect for people at all levels—and the phrase "build fulfilling lives" also reveals a lot about the values that matter to the company.

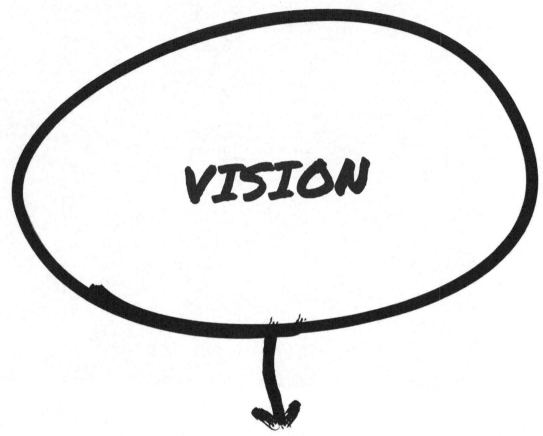

A company's vision articulates the business's medium- to long-term goals and aspirations. Looking years into the future, and if everything goes according to plan, the vision describes how the company will change the world. To be powerful and inspiring, a vision statement should be compelling, meaningful, and boldly ambitious, capturing the essence of why the company exists and what it would make happen if anything were possible. In this chapter, we have slides from Linkedin, GoDaddy, Hootsuite, Nanoheal, and Hubspot.

LINKEDIN

3

Create economic opportunity for every member of the global workforce

LinkedIn's vision will resonate with most people who are interested in helping others get ahead in the world. This is a company that helps improve the lives of others; if you want to do that and make a difference in the world, you should consider working there. This vision statement is commendable in the fact that it's not vague, it *is* encompassing, and it makes sense for a company like LinkedIn to have global ambitions. The background image evokes the LinkedIn network, spanning the globe; it's tasteful, symbolic, and the creativity of the image gives me a sense that the LinkedIn team might share these characteristics too.

GODADDY

OUR VISION

We will radically shift the global economy toward small business by empowering people to easily start, confidently grow and successfully run their own ventures.

GoDaddy

The GoDaddy Vision slide employs powerful words such as *radically, empowering, confidently,* and *successfully* which are exciting and intriguing, yet the vision is solid and matter-of-factual enough to give me the confidence that this company can walk the talk. The photograph itself is engaging and communicates so much; the man's smile is warm and genuine, and I almost feel connected to this person on the other side of the world. It's nicely laid out, and the language is clear and well-written to the very end: "easily start, confidently grow and successfully run". The purpose of the GoDaddy's business feels infused in this slide.

CULTURE
↓
MISSION
↓
VISION
↓
HISTORY
↓
VALUES
↓
THE WAY
WE WORK
AROUND HERE
↓
ONBOARDING
↓
DIVERSITY
+
INCLUSION
↓
FAILURE
↓
TALENT
↓
TRANSPARENCY
↓
FEEDBACK
↓
EMPLOYEE
BENEFITS
↓
MAKE A
DIFFERENCE
↓
BONUS

HOOTSUITE

Vision

Our vision is to revolutionize the customer journey via social.

Hootsuite's vision slide is short, to the point, and is intended to be understood by people who wield two things: a good grasp of what the customer journey means, and a level of fluency and familiarity with social media marketing. Social media seems to be an inevitable part of the future, so it makes sense as being a solid part of a company like Hootsuite's vision.

NANOHEAL

vision

" Be on every device to provide superior user experience by changing the way people live and work with technology. "

Why do we have this **vision**?

CULTURE

MISSION

VISION

HISTORY

VALUES

THE WAY WE WORK AROUND HERE

ONBOARDING

DIVERSITY + INCLUSION

FAILURE

TALENT

TRANSPARENCY

FEEDBACK

EMPLOYEE BENEFITS

MAKE A DIFFERENCE

BONUS

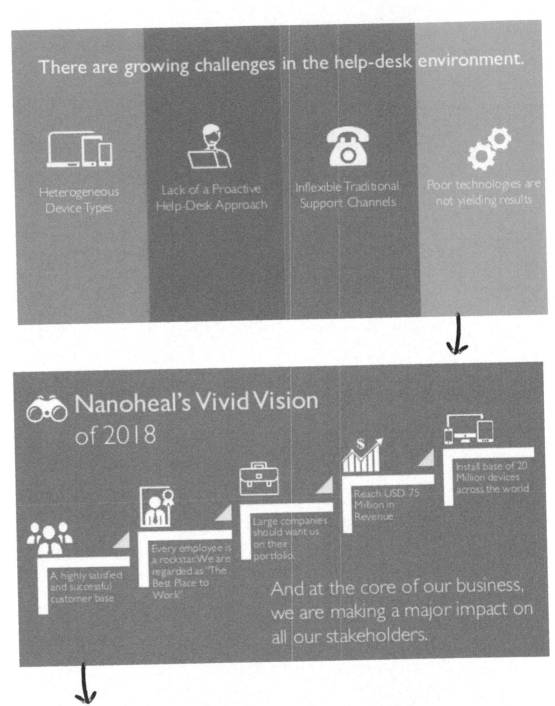

In this set of slides, the Nanoheal team combine their overall vision with a "vivid vision of 2018". This slide is excellent in its thoroughness and in its simplification of the company's major goals for the year. It also wisely shows how each of Nanoheal's five goals are interrelated and must happen chronologically, despite each of them being different.

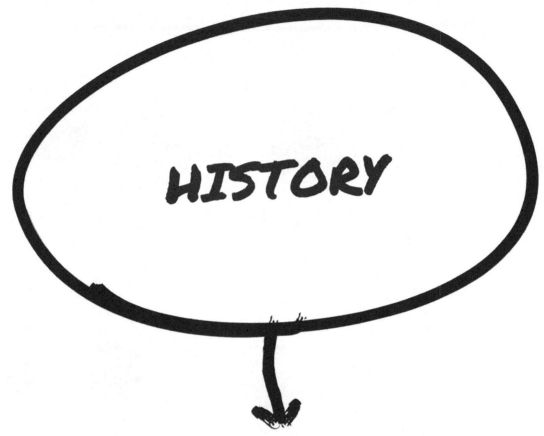

Companies use a History slide in their culture decks to demonstrate how much the company has achieved over time, where the company has come from, the progress that has been made over the years and where the company is heading. In this chapter we have slides from Hootsuite, Hostinger and DoSomething.

DOSOMETHING

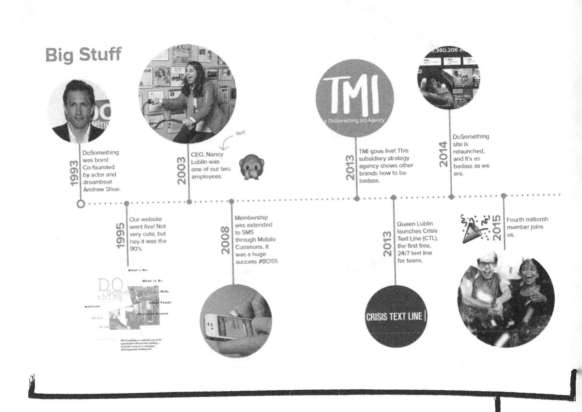

Big Stuff

1993 DoSomething was born! Co-founded by actor and dreamboat Andrew Shue.

2003 CEO, Nancy Lublin was one of our two employees.

2013 TMI goes live! This subsidiary strategy agency shows other brands how to be badass.

2014 DoSomething site is relaunched, and it's as badass as we are.

1995 Our website went live! Not very cute, but hey it was the 90's.

2008 Membership was extended to SMS through Mobile Commons. It was a huge success #BOSS

2013 Queen Lublin launches Crisis Text Line (CTL), the first free, 24/7 text line for teens.

2015 Fourth millionth member joins us.

CRISIS TEXT LINE

The DoSomething history slide is excellent! It's fun, it's personalized, and it's a refreshing way to communicate so many things all at once—not just the history of the company, but the character and personality of the people as well! There is an instant connection with the content and a good balance of words, images, and white space. The first thing that strikes me is the term "Big Stuff" that describes key milestones in the company. There is a childlike energy, and the humor is tongue-in-cheek and self-deprecatory, as exemplified by the "dreamboat" founder and the "monkey say no evil" emoji when mentioning the CEO of only two employees. The vibe is upbeat and positive and the company's progress is evident. The photo of Nancy the CEO on the bike and the two employees celebrating the 4 million[th] member give a telling glimpse into the culture. It comes across as fun, playful, and celebratory—but not, I am sure, without long bouts of hard work in between.

CULTURE
↓
MISSION
↓
VISION
↓
HISTORY
↓
VALUES
↓
THE WAY WE WORK AROUND HERE
↓
ONBOARDING
↓
DIVERSITY + INCLUSION
↓
FAILURE
↓
TALENT
↓
TRANSPARENCY
↓
FEEDBACK
↓
EMPLOYEE BENEFITS
↓
MAKE A DIFFERENCE
↓
BONUS

HOSTINGER

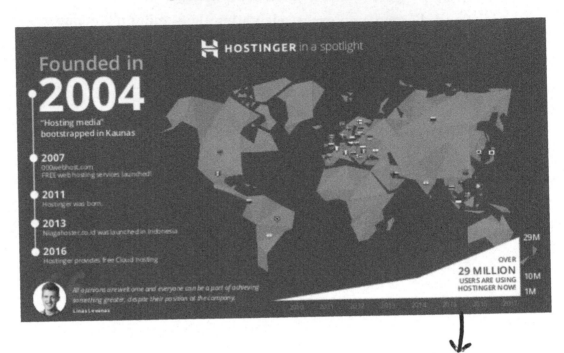

The Hostinger infographic does a good job of communicating the global nature of a bootstrapped media hosting business that has grown to over 29 million users. The company is obviously proud of how far it has come and considers this growth a telling sign of its success and accomplishments—and that is indeed the case. It's also a very effective slide in showing prospective employees a bit of backstory and a glimpse of current events. "All opinions are welcome and everyone can be part of achieving something greater, despite their position at the company" is an apt quote that indicates that there is a level of equality and mutual respect in the company among employees.

HOOTSUITE

History

- In **2008** Hootsuite was born out of Invoke, a digital marketing agency that Ryan founded in 2000.

- For the first year, a seven-person team—one-third of Invoke—grew the
zero-revenue product. (You don't need to be a CFO
to understand that it was tough to make ends meet.)

- But by **2009,** viral growth and investment led us to spin it out as an independent company.

- By **2011,** we entered 'hyper growth,' and have since gone

CULTURE
↓
MISSION
↓
VISION
↓
HISTORY
↓
VALUES
↓
THE WAY
WE WORK
AROUND HERE
↓
ONBOARDING
↓
DIVERSITY
+
INCLUSION
↓
FAILURE
↓
TALENT
↓
TRANSPARENCY
↓
FEEDBACK
↓
EMPLOYEE
BENEFITS
↓
MAKE A
DIFFERENCE
↓
BONUS

Being in hyper growth is kind of like learning to ride a bike down a steep, unpaved hill at breakneck speed:

Everything is flashing past you, there are huge bumps along the way, you HAVE to learn as you go, and all the while, it's a pretty thrilling ride.

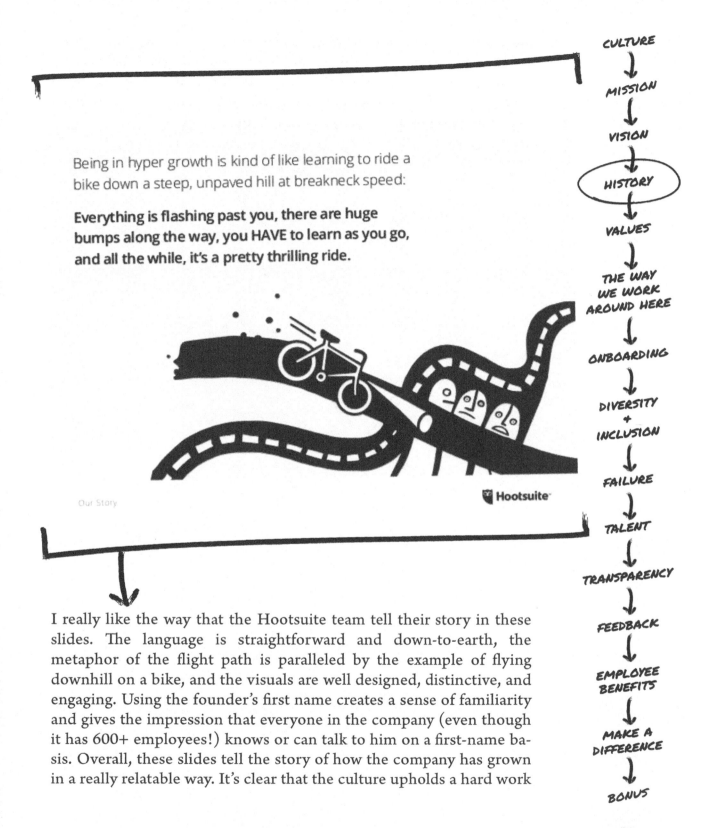

Our Story

Hootsuite

CULTURE
↓
MISSION
↓
VISION
↓
HISTORY
↓
VALUES
↓
THE WAY WE WORK AROUND HERE
↓
ONBOARDING
↓
DIVERSITY + INCLUSION
↓
FAILURE
↓
TALENT
↓
TRANSPARENCY
↓
FEEDBACK
↓
EMPLOYEE BENEFITS
↓
MAKE A DIFFERENCE
↓
BONUS

I really like the way that the Hootsuite team tell their story in these slides. The language is straightforward and down-to-earth, the metaphor of the flight path is paralleled by the example of flying downhill on a bike, and the visuals are well designed, distinctive, and engaging. Using the founder's first name creates a sense of familiarity and gives the impression that everyone in the company (even though it has 600+ employees!) knows or can talk to him on a first-name basis. Overall, these slides tell the story of how the company has grown in a really relatable way. It's clear that the culture upholds a hard work ethic, otherwise the company wouldn't have gotten to the point where it is, but at the same time there is a palpable sense of adventure, as captured in the language about the "pretty thrilling ride". The final slide does a good job of explaining what a prospective employee should expect when joining a company that's undergoing (or about to undergo) "hyper growth".

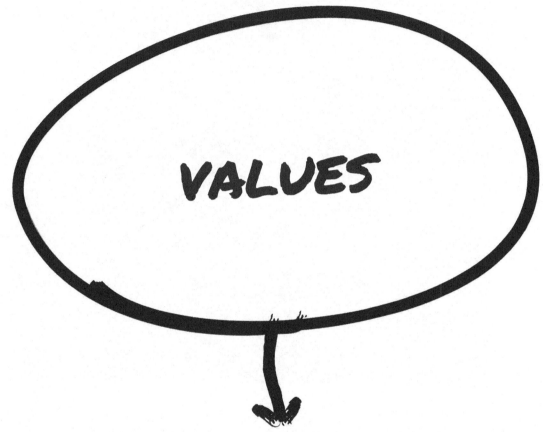

The problem with most companies is that even when they do the hard work of defining their values, they then fail to ensure that their people understand what those values mean to the company. A simple value like *teamwork* can be interpreted in many ways. You may interpret *teamwork* as a group of people working together to achieve a common goal, whereas one of your colleagues may interpret *teamwork* to mean that the team always comes first. You are certainly talking about the same thing and neither person is wrong, but your behaviors and decision-making processes could be radically different. Therefore, the best company decks define what their values mean to the company and are specific about what behaviour is expected from their employees. In this chapter we have slides from LinkedIn, Patreon, Acceleration Partners, IDEO, Buffer, Hubspot, Soundstripe, Runway East and Netflix.

LINKEDIN

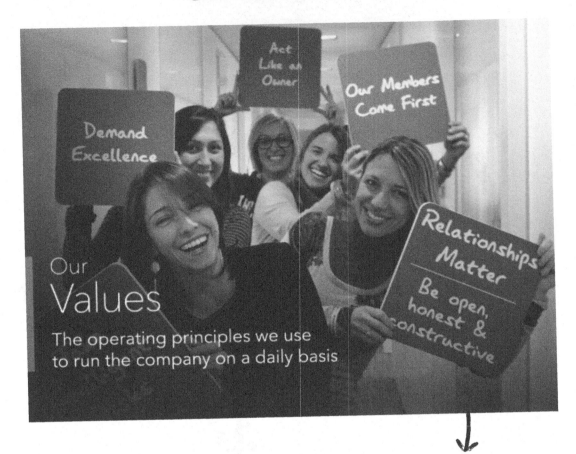

LinkedIn employees' happy faces tell just as much—if not more—than the signs that they're holding up, the signs that broadcast the company's values. It's an intriguing way of showcasing these values. It gives the reader a good sense of the vibrancy, cheerfulness, and youthfulness of the team, and it indicates that they enjoy and are proud of presenting and living up to the values.

☆

DEMAND EXCELLENCE

Our employees are encouraged to lead by example, seek to solve big challenges, set measurable and actionable goals, and continuously learn, iterate and improve. We set a high bar and expect to clear it.

The words *Demand Excellence* reflect a very hard-working culture. LinkedIn is looking for natural leaders who want to be challenged and who are comfortable being held accountable to deliver on those challenges. The slide describes an environment where personal development and improvement are both expected. The language (lead *by example, solve big challenges, set a high bar and expect to clear it*) is impressive and gives tangibility to the phrase *Demand Excellence*. The well-written copy is very clear and powerful. I feel like I get a real sense of the culture from this slide.

CULTURE
↓
MISSION
↓
VISION
↓
HISTORY
↓
⬭ VALUES ⬭
↓
THE WAY
WE WORK
AROUND HERE
↓
ONBOARDING
↓
DIVERSITY
+
INCLUSION
↓
FAILURE
↓
TALENT
↓
TRANSPARENCY
↓
FEEDBACK
↓
EMPLOYEE
BENEFITS
↓
MAKE A
DIFFERENCE
↓
BONUS

Why call them "Core Behaviors" instead of "Core Values?"

Because behaviors are actions you can take and things you can do. In order to build a thriving culture, we live these behaviors and talk about them frequently in our interactions. It is not enough to simply memorize these behaviors. We proactively discuss them and ground all feedback in them.

Most companies have core values. Few companies have cultures that reflect them. You need to be willing to make decisions based on your values, by hiring and promoting people who adhere to them, and letting go of people who do not.

The people of Patreon do a great job of explaining the link between values and behaviors. You can't see a value in action, per say, but you *can* see (and reward) a behaviour. As the company describes its "Core Behaviors", the reader can understand exactly what he or she would need to do to fit in with the Patreon culture. The second paragraph explains the difference between Patreon and most other companies. Because Patreon has defined the specific behaviors it expects to see, its values can really be embedded into the company and lived by the people. This company hires people who resonate with its purpose and work-style, and who adhere to the core behaviors and will fire the people who don't). The company furthermore explains that the decisions that are taken by employees of the company should be based on these key core behaviors thereby giving them the responsibility to get on with their jobs.

Our core behaviors were created by the first two dozen team members at Patreon and have evolved over time. We audit them each year to make sure they still accurately reflect the things our teammates value. You were brought here because we believe you value the things we value. Adhering to these behaviors is how you create a fulfilling career at Patreon.

Here are the 7 things that your teammates care deeply about...

In this slide, Patreon describes how the core behaviors were created and how they are reviewed every year to ensure that they remain relevant. The text explains that employees are hired because they value the same things that the people who already work at Patreon do, and the way to progress and succeed at the company is to embrace and embody the core behaviors.

CULTURE
↓
MISSION
↓
VISION
↓
HISTORY
↓
VALUES
↓
THE WAY
WE WORK
AROUND HERE
↓
ONBOARDING
↓
DIVERSITY
+
INCLUSION
↓
FAILURE
↓
TALENT
↓
TRANSPARENCY
↓
FEEDBACK
↓
EMPLOYEE
BENEFITS
↓
MAKE A
DIFFERENCE
↓
BONUS

Put creators first

Deliver <u>unusual</u> care to creators.

Our business is creators' income and rent checks, so we do not take our responsibility lightly. We exist because of, and in service of, creators. There is a creator behind every text, email, call, request, bug, and payment issue, and we treat them as human beings, not users.

We will fight to keep the human spark in our relationships as we scale. As a business we invest in teams like Community Happiness and Creator Care who are on the front lines taking care of our creators. We revere these teammates on the front lines.

In this slide, it becomes obvious how deeply Patreon cares about the creators (its clients): creators are not just "users", they are real people. The company describes how it supports those creators in their business—a responsibility which the Patreon team doesn't take lightly. The slide demonstrates discipline, humility, and the importance that the company places on retaining its people's humanity. Patreon further explains that the company invests in teams that take care of and put creators first, and that these teams are "revered". The folks at Patreon don't just *say* that they put creators first; they back up what they've said by investing cash, time, effort, and training.

When creators visit our building, we show respect.

When creators perform in our space, we are so quiet you can hear a pin drop. We are not distracted on our devices because we want creators receiving our undivided attention. When creators finish performing, we are so loud that we shake the building.

When a creator leaves Patreon, they should feel like it was the best show of their lives.

The company goes one step further to embed the core behaviours by describing in detail the respect that employees should show to creators, going so far as to describe the feeling that the creators should experience when they leave the company after a performance.

CULTURE
↓
MISSION
↓
VISION
↓
HISTORY
↓
VALUES
↓
THE WAY
WE WORK
AROUND HERE
↓
ONBOARDING
↓
DIVERSITY
+
INCLUSION
↓
FAILURE
↓
TALENT
↓
TRANSPARENCY
↓
FEEDBACK
↓
EMPLOYEE
BENEFITS
↓
MAKE A
DIFFERENCE
↓
BONUS

Core Behaviors Recap

We don't like the term "culture fit" at Patreon. We look for "culture add" and "core behavior fit." We hire people who bring new experiences, backgrounds and perspectives to the table, but you must demonstrate these behaviors to succeed at Patreon.

1. Put creators first
2. Be an energy giver
3. Be candid, always
4. Move fast as hell
5. Seek learning
6. Respect your teammates' time
7. Just fix it

These slides clearly demonstrate that Patreon has done a lot of deep thinking, reflection, and iterating when it comes to its company values and culture. The company makes some interesting statements in these slides, such as stating that its people don't believe in "culture fit" but prefer the terms "culture add" and "core behaviour fit". It's obvious that, in order to work and succeed at Patreon, you don't get the choice of opting out of "adhering" to their core behaviors and values. You have to follow them if you're going to stay part of the company. This makes sense; after all, the point made on the first slide is that "most companies have core values" yet "few companies have cultures that reflect them", and it's hardly a secret that many companies pay lip service to culture without truly living it.

Patreon's core behaviors themselves are stimulating, thought-provoking, and very clear in the expectations that they set out. Putting creators first feels genuinely important to this company, and it's inspiring to read why the Patreon people value creators so much and how the company perceives them: as humans rather than users; as creators, and not as an inconvenience or an unwanted distraction. The company furthermore makes an excellent point by reminding the reader that culture is a work in progress and something that must be continually measured and evaluated to ensure that everyone is upholding it.

ACCELERATION PARTNERS

OUR VISION

Drive the digital marketing industry to be performance-based and change the work-life paradigm.

OUR MISSION

To lead the performance marketing industry though innovation, respect for the brand, exceptional client service and superior results.

CORE VALUES

OWN IT

We step up to the opportunities in front of us, bet on our own abilities and rise to the occasion.

"Owning it" means being proactive and taking accountability for outcomes, even when variables are beyond our control and ambiguity is present. We are confident and accountable in everything we do and are comfortable holding our teammates accountable as well.

EMBRACE RELATIONSHIPS

Relationships advance our personal and professional lives, contributing greatly to our successes.

We focus on long-term outcomes, meaningful relationships and genuine connections with our clients, teammates and partners. We believe that competence and character are fundamental to relationships built on trust and that quality relationships allow us to achieve more.

EXCEL & IMPROVE

We believe that excellence and continuous improvement are inextricably intertwined.

Excellence is a habit created through practice, discipline, and a holistic commitment to quality in all aspects of our lives. We embrace continuous improvement, a love for learning and pushing outside of our comfort zones. We are self-aware and strive to get better in everything that we do.

Acceleration Partners combine their core values, vision and mission on a single slide, which works well as you can recognise that their core values are represented in their mission and vision. Work-life balance is mentioned in the Vision and in the Excel & Improve core value. Trust, quality relationships and connections with clients are mentioned in the Embrace Relationships value, which overlaps with the Mission of "exceptional client service". The company uses a two-stage approach to describe expected behaviors of each value. A one-line positioning statement followed by a more detailed paragraph works well in getting themessage across.

IDEO

Be
Optimistic

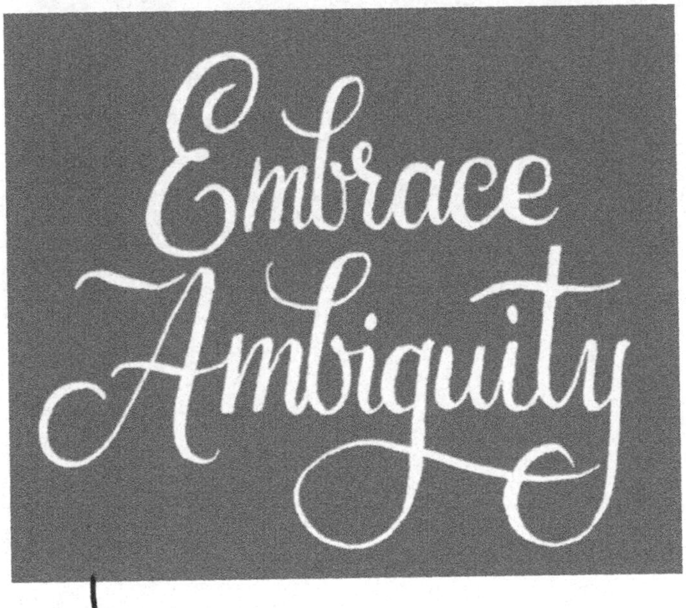

Embrace
Ambiguity

BRETTON PUTTER

CULTURE
↓
MISSION
↓
VISION
↓
HISTORY
↓
VALUES
↓
THE WAY
WE WORK
AROUND HERE
↓
ONBOARDING
↓
DIVERSITY
+
INCLUSION
↓
FAILURE
↓
TALENT
↓
TRANSPARENCY
↓
FEEDBACK
↓
EMPLOYEE
BENEFITS
↓
MAKE A
DIFFERENCE
↓
BONUS

Take
Ownership

Make Others
Successful

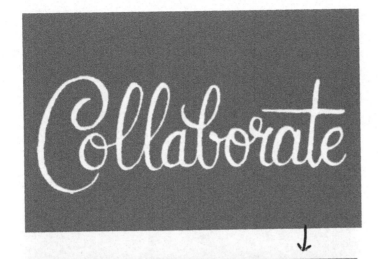

Collaborate

Learn From Failure

CULTURE
↓
MISSION
↓
VISION
↓
HISTORY
↓
VALUES
↓
THE WAY
WE WORK
AROUND HERE
↓
ONBOARDING
↓
DIVERSITY
+
INCLUSION
↓
FAILURE
↓
TALENT
↓
TRANSPARENCY
↓
FEEDBACK
↓
EMPLOYEE
BENEFITS
↓
MAKE A
DIFFERENCE
↓
BONUS

Ideo's slides are very distinctive! There is a consistency, creativity, and uniqueness to the visuals and the fonts used that sets these slides apart from any other company in this document. The text is conversational and memorable, and I think they've got an excellent array of thought-provoking and rather unusual way of wording their values. The values themselves are mature and heavily relationship-oriented. There is a big emphasis on collaboration versus competition; this strikes me as a culture offering its people a balance between the freedom to create and a responsibility to the bigger picture.

BUFFER

buffer

buffer values

words to live
and do business by

open.bufferapp.com/buffer-values/

CHOOSE POSITIVITY
DEFAULT TO TRANSPARENCY
FOCUS ON SELF-IMPROVEMENT
BE A NO-EGO DOER
LISTEN FIRST, THEN LISTEN MORE
COMMUNICATE WITH CLARITY
MAKE TIME TO REFLECT
LIVE SMARTER, NOT HARDER
SHOW GRATITUDE
DO THE RIGHT THING

The Buffer culture, from reading this slide alone, comes across as very appealing. First, the Buffer team describe their values as "words to live and do business by", implying that the living done outside of work is equally important to the company as the work itself. The obvious focus on personal development, respectful relationships, and attitude makes the company feel both fresh and principled. The values speak to me and they make sense and correlate with one another. They have clearly been thought through meticulously and have been expressed in a unique voice, which indicates that Buffer does genuinely care about its values and the kind of culture that it is creating as a company; this isn't just a case of lip service.

CULTURE
↓
MISSION
↓
VISION
↓
HISTORY
↓
(VALUES)
↓
THE WAY
WE WORK
AROUND HERE
↓
ONBOARDING
↓
DIVERSITY
+
INCLUSION
↓
FAILURE
↓
TALENT
↓
TRANSPARENCY
↓
FEEDBACK
↓
EMPLOYEE
BENEFITS
↓
MAKE A
DIFFERENCE
↓
BONUS

Have a focus on self improvement

- You are conscious of your current level of productivity and happiness, and make continual changes to grow

- You have a higher expectation of yourself, than Buffer does of you

- You regularly and deliberately do things that make you feel uncomfortable

- You practice activities and develop habits that will improve your mind and your body

I really appreciate the way that Buffer have detailed the expected behaviors against the "focus on self-improvement" value on the following slide. The detail of this slide demonstrates (once again) that Buffer has thought deeply about the values and what they mean to the company. The company takes a holistic view towards work and personal development. Through this slide, the company informs the reader that it is looking to hire people who are self-aware: Buffer wants employees to be "conscious", "have a higher expectation", want to "grow", "develop habits that will improve your mind and body", and who push the boundaries of what they can consider "uncomfortable" in terms of achievement. I can imagine the interview questions that would be asked to explore these behaviors in a candidate!

HUBSPOT

THE HubSpot CULTURE CODE

1. We commit maniacally to both our **mission** and **metrics**.
2. We look to the long-term and **Solve For The Customer**.
3. We **share openly** and are **remarkably transparent**.
4. We favor **autonomy** and take **ownership**.
5. We believe our best perk is **amazing people**.
6. We dare to be **different** and question the status quo.
7. We recognize that **life is short**.

The "we" element here makes Hubspot feel extremely welcoming, united, familial, and confident in the company's sense of culture and unity. It gives the readers a look at what exists in the company and asks them: can you see yourself among us? I think their use of bold text is tasteful and well-placed, and their wording and their occasional adjectives and adverbs are (Hub)spot-on.

2 | We look to the long-term and **Solve For The Customer**.

SFTC.
Solve for the customer

We don't want to satisfy them, we want to **delight** them.

Our goal is to help them **succeed**.

CULTURE
↓
MISSION
↓
VISION
↓
HISTORY
↓
(VALUES)
↓
THE WAY
WE WORK
AROUND HERE
↓
ONBOARDING
↓
DIVERSITY
+
INCLUSION
↓
FAILURE
↓
TALENT
↓
TRANSPARENCY
↓
FEEDBACK
↓
EMPLOYEE
BENEFITS
↓
MAKE A
DIFFERENCE
↓
BONUS

FOR EVERY DECISION WE SHOULD ASK OURSELVES:

"Selves, what's in it for the customer?"

WAIT. Does "Solve For The Customer" mean just giving more away for free? Wouldn't that delight customers?

NO. To delight customers in the long-term, we have to survive in the short-term.

Because...

Once again, Hubspot's humor comes through in these slides, and alongside the great design, this makes their culture very appealing. What I really like about these slides is that Hubspot takes embedding the values one step further by demonstrating, in a Q&A format, how to use the values in everyday decision making. A key phrase that really jumped out at me is "Solve For The Customer" (the capitalization and bold text tells me this is a key principle in the company and is one that has been thoughtfully examined), which means "delight" the customer (not satisfy) and "help [the customer] succeed". To reiterate the point about solving for the customer and to demonstrate how to explore the value at a deeper level, the company then explains how employees should ask questions regarding this "solving for the customer" process: "For every decision we should ask ourselves, *Selves, what's in it for the customer?*" (I also appreciate the excellent play on words and the humor.)

SOUNDSTRIPE

Our core values are not just fluffy words we put on plaques.

We use our 10 core values as a filter for each and every decision.

Decisions like:

-What does our Soundstripe family interaction look like?

-How do we deal with confrontation?

-When do we quit a project?

-Who do we hire or let go?

-What's our focus?

The people at Soundstripe are crystal clear about the fact that their values have meaning and that the company uses those values as a filter for decision making in the company. In the second slide, the company gives examples; I can easily imagine how the company would use questions like these during their onboarding process to demonstrate the values in action.

CULTURE
↓
MISSION
↓
VISION
↓
HISTORY
↓
(VALUES)
↓
THE WAY
WE WORK
AROUND HERE
↓
ONBOARDING
↓
DIVERSITY
+
INCLUSION
↓
FAILURE
↓
TALENT
↓
TRANSPARENCY
↓
FEEDBACK
↓
EMPLOYEE
BENEFITS
↓
MAKE A
DIFFERENCE
↓
BONUS

Soundstripe Core Values:

Provide all customers with genuine and whimsical care
Confront harsh realities with optimism
Keep it light
Always strive to grow and learn
Develop and practice honest communication
Make it better
Date the model, marry the mission
Be humble and retain a giving and serving heart and mind
Quality over quantity
Done is better than perfect

The words and phrases in the core values list provide insight to the character of the company. "Whimsical care", "Keep it light", "Date the model, not the mission", and "Be humble and retain a giving and serving heart and mind" all reveal that the Soundstripe team has a sense of humor, is not too serious, cares about what they do and has thought about their values.

Date the model. Marry the mission.

If there is a different model or strategy that is discovered or created that better serves our mission, we WILL pivot to it. Even if it means changing the "way we've always done it". When we realize what we've been doing is not the best in serving our mission, even if it's something that we love doing, we insist that our mission will always take precedence over the method, strategy or model.

"I find it so valuable to know that your mission matters more than anything else. If you aren't willing to change your strategies, you won't be able to truly grow to the best of your abilities."

- Chris Small - Marketing Director

CULTURE
↓
MISSION
↓
VISION
↓
HISTORY
↓
VALUES
↓
THE WAY WE WORK AROUND HERE
↓
ONBOARDING
↓
DIVERSITY + INCLUSION
↓
FAILURE
↓
TALENT
↓
TRANSPARENCY
↓
FEEDBACK
↓
EMPLOYEE BENEFITS
↓
MAKE A DIFFERENCE
↓
BONUS

This slide demonstrates the company's wit, openness, and flexibility within their culture—as long as the company is serving the mission. The quote from Chris Small humanizes the slide and reinforces the message.

Overall, Soundstripe emphasizes its dynamic culture in these slides—it's not a static, fluffy, or neglected creature; instead, it's a flexible entity grounded with embedded values that guide and inform every decision. The values are improved perpetually and strategically by examining how they best serve the mission of the company. Though culture is "the way we do things around here", this company is well aware that the phrase isn't the same as "how we've always done it"—the former is in current tense, and the latter is stagnant past tense (limiting progress or creative thinking).

RUNWAY EAST

WELCOME TO THE DEEP END, NEWBIE.

We don't bite, promise. Though, like sharks, we are always in motion, getting shit done, and generally being killer.

We're excited to have you join Runway East - a place that thrives on energy, passion, team-work and smarts. You're here because we know you'll make this place even better. No pressure :)

Everyone says it, but we really do think of ourselves as a family. And like a family, we believe in you 100%, we, like you, won't accept less than your best and we'll be there to come get you when you're lost at 2am "near a big tree" (don't worry, we've all been there).

We've created this pack to give you a crash course in the things that matter most to us. And part of the reason you were hired is because we think they will matter to you, too.

Everything we do is shaped by our values, so drink it in. And welcome to the family.

In this slide, Runway East demonstrates the company's sense of fun and humor. The company recognises that an employee's first day at the company will feel like he or she has been thrown in the deep end; this slide does a great job of welcoming the new employee, setting out what the environment is like, explaining why he or she was hired, and what the company's expectations are ("you'll make this place even better").

At Runway East, we're here to provide a runway for take-off (sorry, but it had to be done): for entrepreneurs, for number-crunchers, for people who will change the world in ways both big and small. At Runway East, we want to help people fly.

We're proud of the spaces we create for flourishing businesses, of the boost we give to brand new ideas, hardened know-how and everything in between. We've boiled down the things we care about into a Runway Flight Code, A C.O.D E., to be precise: We put our *Community* first, we're *Open*, we give a *Damn*, and at our core, we're *Entrepreneurs*.

OUR VALUES DRIVE US

COMMUNITY FIRST

Our job is to get our fantastic startups where they want to be. At the end of the day, their success is our success.

WE'RE OPEN

We're honest, encouraging and hungry to learn. Every mistake we make is a chance to make what we do better.

GIVE A DAMN

We care fiercely about the projects and people we work with. We thrive on challenges, on excitement and on Getting Shit Done.

ENTREPRENEURS

To us, entrepreneurial means taking the initiative. We're a group of people driven by creativity, by the ability to spot opportunities, solutions and new ideas – and by the excitement of trying to get those ideas off the ground.

CULTURE
↓
MISSION
↓
VISION
↓
HISTORY
↓
VALUES
↓
THE WAY
WE WORK
AROUND HERE
↓
ONBOARDING
↓
DIVERSITY
+
INCLUSION
↓
FAILURE
↓
TALENT
↓
TRANSPARENCY
↓
FEEDBACK
↓
EMPLOYEE
BENEFITS
↓
MAKE A
DIFFERENCE
↓
BONUS

Seriously though, our values drive us.
But talk is cheap. Let's dig down into action.

COMMUNITY FIRST

We help make great things happen. We do that by knowing what our startups want - from the overarching dream to the everyday excitement.

We keep things running smoothly. We put ourselves in our members' shoes constantly, and we don't wait to be asked to fix a problem. They love us because we're on their team, we share their problems, their victories, and we're always ready to dive in.

After all, to make big, important things happen, a whole lot of tiny important things need to happen. We consider ourselves kings and queens of the tiny important things.

COMMUNITY FIRST IN ACTION

We don't want to be like a lot of our big corporate competitors. It's important to us that we always act as humans first, and as a business second.

A while ago, one of our loyal members was going through a tough financial period - a common thing for start ups. Their success is our success, so instead of turfing them out for not being able to pay their rent, we agreed that they could stay in their office, we supported their work, and delayed payment for 6 months until they were back up on their feet.

Through sheer determination, they managed to turn their business around in that 6 months and are still one of our members now. We couldn't be happier for them.

We gave them the chance without knowing whether they would ever be able to pay us back, but we have faith in our members, and know a good thing when we see it.

Runway East details its values, what it does for its community of clients and what the values mean to the company. I really like the phrase "kings and queens of the tiny important things" because it reinforces the need to be able to deliver operational excellence for the community. The Runway East people detail what's expected against each value and go a further step by giving a past example of that value in action within the company (in this case demonstrating that loyalty was rewarded with consideration and flexibility). This is a powerful way of bringing the values to life for a new employee.

NETFLIX

The *actual* company values,
as opposed to the
nice-sounding values,
are shown by who gets
rewarded, promoted, or let go

This Netflix slide communicates a certain ruthlessness and level of expectation in the culture towards its people. The emphasis on "nice-sounding" values refers to what most other companies do, which is to pay lip service to values but to not really live them. There is a strict, disciplined feel to these slides.

CULTURE
↓
MISSION
↓
VISION
↓
HISTORY
↓
VALUES
↓
THE WAY
WE WORK
AROUND HERE
↓
ONBOARDING
↓
DIVERSITY
+
INCLUSION
↓
FAILURE
↓
TALENT
↓
TRANSPARENCY
↓
FEEDBACK
↓
EMPLOYEE
BENEFITS
↓
MAKE A
DIFFERENCE
↓
BONUS

Actual company values are the *behaviors* and *skills* that are *valued* in fellow employees

Netflix communicates in clear and simple language how living the values, the actual behaviors, and the skills that are demonstrated by fellow employees will all help to get a new employee rewarded and promoted (or fired, if he or she fails to live up to the values). In the second slide, the company encourages new employees to be aware of how the longer-term employees are behaving, and to use them as role models and look out for the behaviors in action.

At Netflix, we particularly value the following nine behaviors and skills in our colleagues...

...meaning we hire and promote people who demonstrate these nine

For reference Netflix nine behaviors and skills are

1. JUDGEMENT
2. PRODUCTIVITY
3. CREATIVITY
4. INTELLIGENCE
5. HONESTY
6. COMMUNICATION
7. SELFLESSNESS
8. RELIABILITY
9. PASSION

CULTURE
↓
MISSION
↓
VISION
↓
HISTORY
↓
VALUES
↓
THE WAY
WE WORK
AROUND HERE
↓
ONBOARDING
↓
DIVERSITY
+
INCLUSION
↓
FAILURE
↓
TALENT
↓
TRANSPARENCY
↓
FEEDBACK
↓
EMPLOYEE
BENEFITS
↓
MAKE A
DIFFERENCE
↓
BONUS

Selflessness

You seek what is best for Netflix, rather than best for yourself or your group

You are ego-less when searching for the best ideas

You make time to help colleagues

You share information openly and proactively

Netflix clearly defines what's expected by the word *selfless*, removing any room for misinterpretation or doubt. You are selfless and your focus, should you wish to join Netflix, is on the company, finding the best ideas, helping colleagues and information sharing. The four descriptions are clear and straightforward, resulting in a simple process within the company when it comes to being able to hold yourself or a colleague accountable for something, or being able to interview for this selflessness.

Culture develops when decisions that are made prove to be successful, and the thinking that went into those decisions becomes embedded into "the way we do things around here". The companies in this chapter give a fascinating insight into how the company ticks, why it does what it does, what makes the company unique, and why if you are a prospective employee or candidate you should seriously consider working there. In this chapter we have slides from Asana, Nanigans, Morey Creative Studios, Hotjar, Next Jump, LinkedIn, ROI Online, Netflix, eShares, Nordstrom, Hubspot, Hootsuite and Handy.

ASANA

Distributed responsibility

Instead of having all decisions flow through management, we distribute responsibility as evenly as possible. Everyone at Asana has clearly defined Areas of Responsibility, for which they are the ultimate decision maker.

This is a new approach to workplace empowerment and is why Asana scores in 99th percentile of employee engagement for our industry and is consistently rated 5 out of 5 on the popular review site, Glassdoor.

TEAM OF PEERS

Working in episodes

We organize our company calendar into **Episodes**.

Approaching our work in focused periods of time helps us prioritize, keeps us accountable, and ensures we're always moving forward.

We plan and define goals before the start of each episode during **Roadmap Week**.

Every team sets goals for each episode called **Key Results**.

Each Episode has two special weeks: **Polish Week** and **Grease Week**.

WORK HARD

The content of these Asana slides is very intriguing. The folks at Asana have a different management style than that of most companies; Asana calls this "workplace empowerment". In this realm, each employee is a decision maker for his or her own area of responsibility, which is clearly defined by the company. This in-built autonomy, the idea of distributed responsibility, high employee engagement, and being an empowered decision maker in your role are all very appealing characteristics. The first slide gives statistics to back up the company's claims and is written in the plural first person, using "we" and "our", which helps to build rapport with the reader. The idea of a "team of peers" also feels personalized and genuine. The company does a great job in the second slide of describing the Asana sprint process using the descriptive word *episodes* to describe how the process works. These "episodes" help the company prioritize and keeps employees and teams accountable.

CULTURE
↓
MISSION
↓
VISION
↓
HISTORY
↓
VALUES
↓
THE WAY WE WORK AROUND HERE
↓
ONBOARDING
↓
DIVERSITY + INCLUSION
↓
FAILURE
↓
TALENT
↓
TRANSPARENCY
↓
FEEDBACK
↓
EMPLOYEE BENEFITS
↓
MAKE A DIFFERENCE
↓
BONUS

SHARED
EXPERIENCES
AT **nanigans**

"Everyone works really hard to carry their own weight and make sure they're pushing things forward as much as they can. But there's also lightheartedness, poking fun at stuff and joking around. It's **that good mix** of really hard work and having a good laugh at the same time."

– Campaign Management

nanigans

In these slides, the Nanigans team describes the six shared experiences that the company is looking for from its employees. With the "Work hard, play hard" motto, the company wants to show new employees that it does expect results, but it is also a fun place to work. The company uses a quote against each shared experience to communicate what that particular value or expectation means, and consequently what's expected from employees. Personally, I interpret the "carry their own weight" and be "pushing things forward" values to mean that a new employee must be able to hit the ground running and get up to speed with their new role as quickly as possible in order to not be a drag on the company.

MOREY CREATIVE STUDIOS

Result matter more than
the number of hours we work.

We understand what we are trying to achieve
and measure our success against that.

It's a shame that there's a glaring typo in Morey's slide ("result matter" instead of "results matter"), but it is otherwise an extremely powerful message that shows that the company is fresh and forward-thinking. Most employers pay their people to work a certain number of hours per week regardless of their performance during those hours. Instead of clock-watching, they are focused on getting the job done and creating the results that are essential for moving the business forward. The text on this slide backs this notion by being clear that the company knows what it is trying to achieve and knows how to measure success. This is a distinctive message and key differentiator for Morey.

CULTURE
↓
MISSION
↓
VISION
↓
HISTORY
↓
VALUES
↓
(THE WAY WE WORK AROUND HERE)
↓
ONBOARDING
↓
DIVERSITY + INCLUSION
↓
FAILURE
↓
TALENT
↓
TRANSPARENCY
↓
FEEDBACK
↓
EMPLOYEE BENEFITS
↓
MAKE A DIFFERENCE
↓
BONUS

HOTJAR

Weekly Structure

In order to better align our focus / meeting / planning hours across all teams and maximize opportunities for communication, we have set out rough guidelines to structure our working week. These guidelines are not set in stone but are meant to help us schedule calls and collaborate better. All team members are free to set out their own work week, keeping in mind the guidelines set out below:

Mondays: Call heavy days! We have our planning meetings, 1-1s, sync calls, etc., on Monday. People are likely to be in meetings for the large part of the day so they might be a bit slower when it comes to responding to messages.

Tuesdays: Focus days! Tuesdays are the generally the most productive working days of the week. Having a focus day on Tuesday allows each team member to focus more on their sprints. We try to avoid having regular scheduled meetings on Tuesdays unless they are project centric. This doesn't mean that communication or cross team collaboration is off the table - we can't work without speaking to each other, neither do we want to encourage this! Other team members are less likely to be tied up in meetings on Tuesdays.

Wednesdays: No meeting Wednesdays! We never have scheduled calls on Wednesdays unless it is an emergency. People will jump on quick calls as necessary to collaborate, and still communicate via Hipchat / Email.

Thursdays + Fridays: All our 'big' meetings are scheduled for these days - weekly demos, monthly meetings, Leadership planning, etc. How call-busy people are will depends on the week we are in during the month.

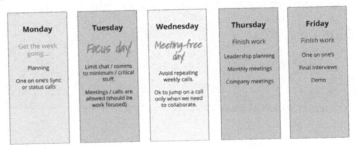

Monday	Tuesday	Wednesday	Thursday	Friday
Get the week going...	Focus day!	Meeting-free day!	Finish work	Finish work
Planning	Limit chat / comms to minimum / critical stuff.	Avoid repeating weekly calls.	Leadership planning	One on one's
One on one's Sync or status calls	Meetings / calls are allowed (should be work focused)	Ok to jump on a call only when we need to collaborate.	Monthly meetings	Final Interviews
			Company meetings	Demo

This is a really interesting approach to the working week. Although I've spent a lot of time over the years looking into different approaches to productivity, rarely have I seen a company-wide approach like this. It's impressive and clearly well thought through, acknowledging both the rhythm of the week (e.g. helping people to ease in on Mondays via planning and status update calls) and the detrimental impact that things like meetings can have. It's great to see that they say that team members are free to work however they want, but it's also clear that they've learned from experience here.

Meetups

Sara Bent
Last modified Mar 28, 2018

As a fully remote team, we're spread out across several continents and the benefits of this, for us, outweigh the challenges. However, we know how much worth comes from getting to know each other in person. Our team meets up several times a year for this reason, be it with the entire company or for smaller team meetups. While attendance is highly encouraged, it's never compulsory. We know that team members might have other things happening in their lives to prevent them from coming. Travel to and from, and all expenses for these meetups are paid for by the company.

We generally travel Monday (departure) and Friday (return) in order to have 3 full days together. People are welcome to extend their trip on either side to make the most of the location they're heading to - the Holiday budget is there to be used!

Company Retreats

Twice a year - in summer and winter - we bring our entire company together, at a different location each time. We choose the location based on weather at the time of year, and how easy it is to fly people in from so many different locations. It's a chance to catch up with the entire team, to meet new team members who have joined since the last retreat, and for all to get to know each other, have fun, and to learn together.

Team Meet-ups

We also meet up once or twice a year in our smaller teams, for a week of dedicated work. It's great to use the time working together from the same space to collaborate on big projects. Depending on the department, these meet-ups might take the form of hackathons, docuthons.... Any form that works best for the team and their work.

Hotjar understands how important it is for their remote team to come together, connect and share experiences, so they take their people on a non-compulsory retreat twice a year and arrange additional with mini-retreats during the year. The company puts a huge amount of effort, time and money into bringing its people together, where the aim is to create a great bonding and learning experience for everybody.

CULTURE
↓
MISSION
↓
VISION
↓
HISTORY
↓
VALUES
↓
THE WAY
WE WORK
AROUND HERE
↓
ONBOARDING
↓
DIVERSITY
+
INCLUSION
↓
FAILURE
↓
TALENT
↓
TRANSPARENCY
↓
FEEDBACK
↓
EMPLOYEE
BENEFITS
↓
MAKE A
DIFFERENCE
↓
BONUS

NEXT JUMP

It's so interesting that the image from this slide *could* be of a celebrity couple at an awards show, but in fact it is actually depicting what the company terms a "Talking Partnership." There is a close friendship and visible intimacy between the two people that arguable the majority of individuals have probably never experienced at work and never will. Yet the context of this slide is purely professional and all about leadership development. As the text explains, the TP program is a co-mentoring strategy which takes the Boston Globe's insight regarding the efficiency gained from working in a pair, and applies it to the Next Jump workplace. The Next Jump Talking Partners (TPs) meet daily to share their issues, frustrations, and thoughts about the coming day before they start work—essentially, this is a deliberate release valve. The photo also indicates that the company invests in things like galas or possibly awards nights; the image definitely wasn't captured during a typical workday!

The flow diagram on the right shows:

CULTURE → MISSION → VISION → HISTORY → VALUES → THE WAY WE WORK AROUND HERE → ONBOARDING → DIVERSITY + INCLUSION → FAILURE → TALENT → TRANSPARENCY → FEEDBACK → EMPLOYEE BENEFITS → MAKE A DIFFERENCE → BONUS

There's quite a lot of information about the company from this one slide. The branding is prominent, as it is in every slide so far, and the photograph depicts a situational workshop which looks like a standard meeting but which actually, as the text explains, is specifically geared towards the goal of scaling senior level mentoring within the organization through the process of coaching situational decision making. Situational workshops are weekly meetings composed of five people: two different pairs of Talking Partners, plus a more experienced colleague acting as the coach. During each workshop, every one of the four Next Jumper TPs takes their turn to voice a current dilemma or challenging situation they've found themselves in during that week. They then receive feedback and coaching around the issue, provided by the workshop coach; this person asks, among other questions: "What are you learning about yourself in having this problem?" The situation is obviously acknowledged as a valuable learning opportunity.

Next Jump describes situational workshops as "coaching at scale," stating that these workshops enable the company "to develop leaders at all levels." This is pretty rare; usually, coaching is reserved for the 5% of people within the company who have been identified as "high potentials" or "elite performers"; the leaders at Next Jump, however, are convinced that their strategy is part of what sets them apart and that it is well worth the investment of their time, energy, and money. From the slide, it's also apparent that the company is health conscious; there's a bowl of fruit (rather than biscuits or cookies) on the table, and everyone has water to drink (although it is a real shame that the company is using single-use plastic bottles rather than reusable water bottles; perhaps this is a missed opportunity?).

ABOVE WATERLINE

CULTURE
INITIATIVES

BELOW WATERLINE

REVENUE
INITIATIVES

CULTURE
↓
MISSION
↓
VISION
↓
HISTORY
↓
VALUES
↓
THE WAY
WE WORK
AROUND HERE
↓
ONBOARDING
↓
DIVERSITY
+
INCLUSION
↓
FAILURE
↓
TALENT
↓
TRANSPARENCY
↓
FEEDBACK
↓
EMPLOYEE
BENEFITS
↓
MAKE A
DIFFERENCE
↓
BONUS

Bill Gore, the founder of W.L. Gore and Associates, came up with this idea of the waterline to describe a business's area of danger. Regarding the ship, the waterline is the point where the ship's hull meets the surface of the water. And while autonomy and creativity are encouraged, associates at Gore need to first consult with a fellow associate before going "below the waterline" and potentially damaging the company. In a similar way, Next Jump uses the waterline to separate its culture initiatives from its revenue-driven initiatives. Employees are expected to spend 50% of their time on culture-related activities and 50% of their time on revenue initiatives. Culture initiatives are allowed to fail as long as they don't threaten the "below the waterline" revenue initiatives. Next Jump uses its culture initiatives as a "safe space" training ground to develop its people's leadership skills.

LINKEDIN

Company All Hands

Our bi-weekly Company All Hands sets the tone for open, honest and constructive communication — one of our core values. It's also a lot of fun, too.

InDay

InDay is a day at LinkedIn where employees take all or part of the day off, once a month, from our regular work to explore new ideas, hack with friends, volunteer for special causes, invest in ourselves or whatever inspires us.

These two slides give a window of insight into two of the LinkedIn's internal culture development programs: the All Hands Meeting and the InDay. LinkedIn's bi-weekly All Hands Company meetings are meant to ensure that everyone is on the same page and that the company can sidestep those all-too-common communication problems that can so often plague high-growth companies. The slide talks about setting the tone for the transparency in the company with "open, honest, and constructive communications", which reinforces one of the company's core values. The slide image demonstrates that these meetings can also be a lot of fun.

LinkedIn encourages its team to take an "Investment Day" (or InDay for short), which is a half or full day off, provided once a month, for their employees to do something that is inspiring. It's a day for employees to focus on themselves, the company, and the world. This slide demonstrates that the company understands the importance of investing in its employees in order for them to be able to invest in themselves. Each month has a theme (such as *giving back, relationships, wellness and play*), and employees can bond and enjoy different experiences outside of the typical office environment. The photo seems to depict

CULTURE

↓

MISSION

↓

VISION

↓

HISTORY

↓

VALUES

↓

THE WAY
WE WORK
AROUND HERE

↓

ONBOARDING

↓

DIVERSITY
+
INCLUSION

↓

FAILURE

↓

TALENT

↓

TRANSPARENCY

↓

FEEDBACK

↓

EMPLOYEE
BENEFITS

↓

MAKE A
DIFFERENCE

↓

BONUS

a team of LinkedIn employees who used one of their InDays to go climbing, which looks fun, adventurous, physically invigorating, and could possibly even be an event that raised money for charity. Such activities—such as the monthly day off from regular work, devoted to developing ideas, doing hacks, volunteering, or investing in what inspires and matters—show me that this is a culture that cares about its people.

ROI Online

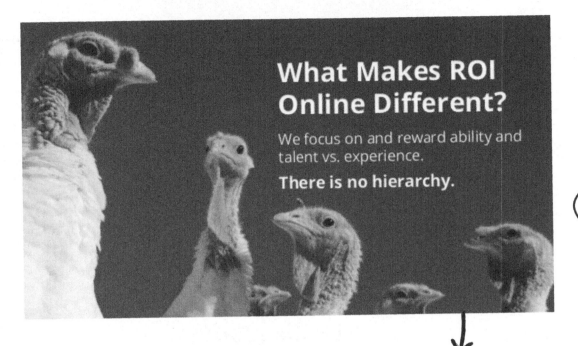

CULTURE
↓
MISSION
↓
VISION
↓
HISTORY
↓
VALUES
↓
THE WAY
WE WORK
AROUND HERE
↓
ONBOARDING
↓
DIVERSITY
+
INCLUSION
↓
FAILURE
↓
TALENT
↓
TRANSPARENCY
↓
FEEDBACK
↓
EMPLOYEE
BENEFITS
↓
MAKE A
DIFFERENCE
↓
BONUS

I appreciate the humor in this slide. The folks at ROI Online are clearly not turkeys. But it shows that the company doesn't have a hierarchical management structure and they look for talent and ability over experience. If you have the right attitude and ability, you have a great chance of progressing at this company and you'll probably have a lot of fun along the way.

NETFLIX

We're a *team*, not a family

We're like a **pro sports team**,
not a kid's recreational team

Netflix leaders
hire, develop and cut **smartly**,
so we have stars in every position

NETFLIX

Once again, Netflix tells it like it is—this is a bullshit-free zone where you won't be around for long if you don't pull your weight. The direct, no-holds-barred tone of this slide feels like it's probably designed to be deliberately intimidating, sorting out the people who will thrive in the pro sports type of environment from the people who won't.

Athletes in pro sports teams are well paid. Pro sports teams expect their athletes to train hard, develop their skills, unite as a team, and learn from their mistakes. The best teams learn how to win and become recognized as stars; this slide communicates the high esteem—and expectations—to which Netflix holds every employee, terming its team as "stars". If, however, you as an employee are not able to fit in with the team, or if you are not able to deliver to the team's expectations, you will be let go. Not for the first time, Netflix deliberately states that they "cut" or fire people who don't perform at the pro level.

Little leaguers, steer clear. Only hardworking stars need apply...

CULTURE
↓
MISSION
↓
VISION
↓
HISTORY
↓
VALUES
↓
THE WAY WE WORK AROUND HERE
↓
ONBOARDING
↓
DIVERSITY + INCLUSION
↓
FAILURE
↓
TALENT
↓
TRANSPARENCY
↓
FEEDBACK
↓
EMPLOYEE BENEFITS
↓
MAKE A DIFFERENCE
↓
BONUS

ESHARES

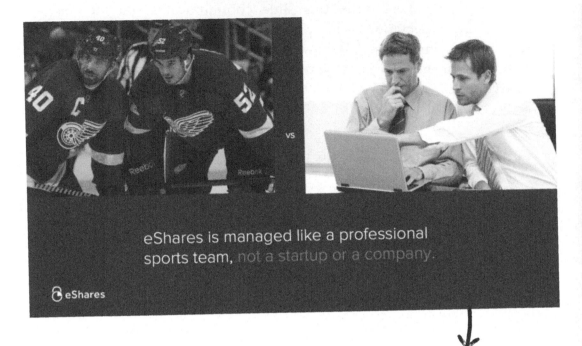

eShares is managed like a professional sports team, not a startup or a company.

🔒 eShares

I find the two visuals to be quite telling; the hockey players are huddling and seem to be collaborating, plotting, or conspiring together, which (even at just a glance) exudes a sense of camaraderie in a fast-paced and literally high-speed environment where, just like in a startup, you must master the art of "skating to where the puck will be".

The second picture shows one man taking charge and pointing out something to the other man; this second man looks anxious or confused—he is certainly less confident and knowledgeable, at least at this moment in time, than his counterpart. The latter picture is also far more formal and structured: shirt and tie, laptop, conference table, bland background, close-trimmed hair and shaved face, etc.

The company really makes a statement by stating on the slide that it is not like any other company that you, as a prospective candidate or employee, will have worked at before. This is an intriguing and evocative statement, and sets the reader up for the next slides in the deck.

No titles. Just positions.

We are all defined as eShares employees.

We play positions like "Sales", "Product", "Dev".

We are not defined with titles like "Vice President" or "Senior Analyst".

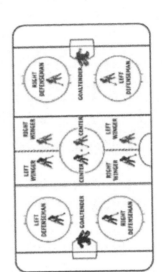

CULTURE

↓

MISSION

↓

VISION

↓

HISTORY

↓

VALUES

↓

THE WAY
WE WORK
AROUND HERE

↓

ONBOARDING

↓

DIVERSITY
+
INCLUSION

↓

FAILURE

↓

TALENT

↓

TRANSPARENCY

↓

FEEDBACK

↓

EMPLOYEE
BENEFITS

↓

MAKE A
DIFFERENCE

↓

BONUS

"Org chart" is our current formation.

The "org chart" changes depending on the goals of the organization.

We change the org chart frequently (sometimes every month).

People move groups and change managers frequently.

People are tied to positions, not titles.

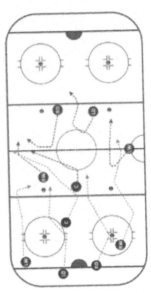

Teams are limited to 8.

Amazon calls it the "two-pizza rule."

Nobody is allowed to have more than 8 direct reports.

If a team has to grow past 8, then it splits.

It is impossible to "empire-build."

CULTURE
↓
MISSION
↓
VISION
↓
HISTORY
↓
VALUES
↓
THE WAY WE WORK AROUND HERE
↓
ONBOARDING
↓
DIVERSITY + INCLUSION
↓
FAILURE
↓
TALENT
↓
TRANSPARENCY
↓
FEEDBACK
↓
EMPLOYEE BENEFITS
↓
MAKE A DIFFERENCE
↓
BONUS

So how different is the culture at this company? At eShares, employees do not carry titles. Job positions are defined based on the function being delivered. The org chart can and will change, the manager can and will change, and teams are kept compact and are never allowed to become larger than 8 people in number. This "no org chart" structure is bold and unusual. I doubt that most people would be comfortable dealing with the ambiguity and uncertainty of working in an organization where the current formation was constantly shifting and changing—on the other hand, it might be right up your alley and exactly what you're looking for. Whatever the case, this material suggests that this is a truly different and agile company culture.

NORDSTROM

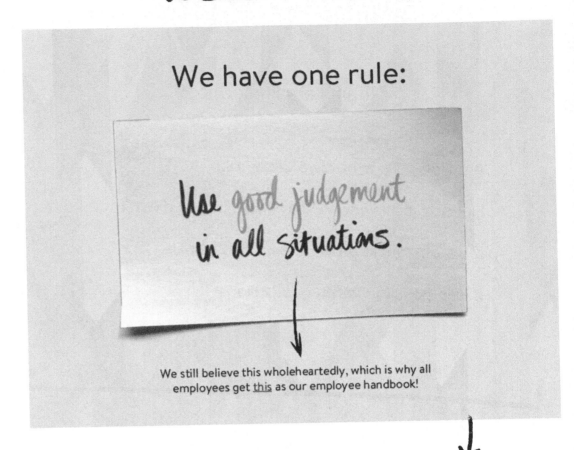

Nordstrom's slide is simple, straightforward, and so very visually elegant. I really like this because it implies that responsibility and autonomy are key factors to an employee's success.

Hubspot

	THEN	NOW
FOCUS	Pension	**Purpose**
NEED	Good Boss	**Great Colleagues**
HOURS	9-5	**Whenever**
WORKPLACE	Office	**Wherever**
TENURE	Whole Career	**Whatever**

Hubspot does a great job in bluntly contrasting traditional work with its own unique and people-centric model. The Hubspot team are aware of the past but are also grounded in the present. Employees' old priorities—securing a good boss, a 9-5, an office-based job, a pension, and a job for life—have been replaced by the much fresher and more flexible and ambiguous work lifestyle of "Whenever, Wherever, Whatever", along with an enforced emphasis on purpose and collegiate relationships. As with many of the cultures highlighted in this document, the focus here is on a much more flexible way of working. I think this would appeal to individuals (particularly millennials) who are looking for flexibility, autonomy, responsibility, and the opportunity to build meaningful relationships in a purposeful job.

CULTURE
↓
MISSION
↓
VISION
↓
HISTORY
↓
VALUES
↓
THE WAY
WE WORK
AROUND HERE
↓
ONBOARDING
↓
DIVERSITY
+
INCLUSION
↓
FAILURE
↓
TALENT
↓
TRANSPARENCY
↓
FEEDBACK
↓
EMPLOYEE
BENEFITS
↓
MAKE A
DIFFERENCE
↓
BONUS

HOOTSUITE

CULTURE
↓
MISSION
↓
VISION
↓
HISTORY
↓
VALUES
↓
(THE WAY
WE WORK
AROUND HERE)
↓
ONBOARDING
↓
DIVERSITY
+
INCLUSION
↓
FAILURE
↓
TALENT
↓
TRANSPARENCY
↓
FEEDBACK
↓
EMPLOYEE
BENEFITS
↓
MAKE A
DIFFERENCE
↓
BONUS

Yup, B.S.U. is an acronym for 'blow shit up'.

In the early days of Hootsuite, the phrase was widely used
by Ryan, as a motivational mantra to get people excited
about what they were working on: "Let's blow shit up!"

("Let's build some internet people!"
was the other phrase he used a lot back
then, but didn't stick in the same way.)

Our Culture · #BSU

Hootsuite

CULTURE DECKS DECODED

Before we knew it, "Let's blow shit up!" was being used by all departments across the company—in emails, chats, parties, even town halls, and by everyone, from the newest intern to our top VPs and executives.

And eventually, in true fashion of a social media company, we made into a viral hashtag: #BSU

Peeps
BLOW SHIT UP BSU
BSU
BSU BSU
BSU BSU
Hootsuite BSU
BSU BSU

Our Culture · #BSU

🦉 Hootsuite

CULTURE
↓
MISSION
↓
VISION
↓
HISTORY
↓
VALUES
↓
(THE WAY WE WORK AROUND HERE)
↓
ONBOARDING
↓
DIVERSITY + INCLUSION
↓
FAILURE
↓
TALENT
↓
TRANSPARENCY
↓
FEEDBACK
↓
EMPLOYEE BENEFITS
↓
MAKE A DIFFERENCE
↓
BONUS

Our Culture · #BSU

4 Reasons:

1. **#BSU is a pillar of our language and culture**.

2. **It has lots of energy behind it**. Like many of us here.

3. **It's limitless**. There are no limits to how much or how far you can 'blow shit up.' And it applies to all of us who work here. Whether it's an amazing line of code or a new product or marketing campaign, we can all take our own project and blow it up!

4. Finally, 'blow shit up,' is **inherently disruptive in nature**, just like we are.

CULTURE

MISSION

VISION

HISTORY

VALUES

THE WAY
WE WORK
AROUND HERE

ONBOARDING

DIVERSITY
+
INCLUSION

FAILURE

TALENT

TRANSPARENCY

FEEDBACK

EMPLOYEE
BENEFITS

MAKE A
DIFFERENCE

BONUS

Work out loud

We strive to constantly give each other visibility into the bigger picture.

Keep open doors

We have an open door policy for everyone, no matter what position. Our offices therefore have no walls or barriers (physically or metaphorically).

Set visible, big picture goals

Knowing what others are doing and seeing big picture goals helps us better support each other and share a greater sense of purpose.

These Hootsuite slides are a hoot! They do a great job of breaking down the "what", "when", "who", "how", and "why" of the whole #BSU mantra. The first two slides are funny, surprising, and (as the latter slides proudly note) disruptive. BSU is edgy, irreverent, cool, and revolutionary. It's great to hear the story of how the term BSU made its way into the company's vernacular and culture (#BSU) at Hootsuite, and the final two slides give a robust explanation of why BSU has stuck and how it translates into the team's behaviors. The style of the slides is energetic, playful, and professional—much how I'd envision the company's employees to be. Anybody who wants to work at Hootsuite should be comfortable metaphorically "blowing shit up". If you're not, you can self-select yourself out of the hiring process without wasting anyone's time.

HANDY

What this means daily in practice:

If an email comes in and you're about to enter the elevator to go home, if you can answer at that moment and unblock a junior team member or make an important decision, take action then and there. Avoid the mindset that "this email will still be in my inbox tomorrow, so it can wait a day."

—

If you can push yourself a bit more on a Thursday to push code, knowing on Fridays we don't push, then do it. Don't wait until Monday. Customers and pros will be better off 3 days earlier.

—

If you are working on an data analysis, and can get it done today rather than tomorrow, that means your business partner can make a decision earlier which can drive a policy or process change sooner.

42

On this slide, Handy emphasises that being tenacious and going the extra mile matter today and everyday—especially when your actions, no matter how big or small, have an impact on other people. The replacement of the struck-through word "your" in the visual with "our" is a choice that highlights how the company prioritizes a culture of "we" over "me" and the copy clearly suggests that if you can put in the extra time—whether that is five minutes to send an email or a few extra hours to finish off a bigger piece of work—you should. The text does a great job making this slide relevant to the reader, giving three different examples, at least one of which will be personally pertinent and should resonate with everybody in the company.

CULTURE
↓
MISSION
↓
VISION
↓
HISTORY
↓
VALUES
↓
THE WAY WE WORK AROUND HERE
↓
ONBOARDING
↓
DIVERSITY + INCLUSION
↓
FAILURE
↓
TALENT
↓
TRANSPARENCY
↓
FEEDBACK
↓
EMPLOYEE BENEFITS
↓
MAKE A DIFFERENCE
↓
BONUS

The first challenge with onboarding new hires is to ensure that they hit the ground running and are productive from day one. Apart from the basic training, it's important for the new hire to get their head around the invisible currents of the company culture – the group dynamics, personalities, power structures, decision-making norms and any non-obvious hierarchies that exist. A buddy/mentor is an excellent way to help the new employee understand what the currents are and identify who the relevant people are to talk to. The most successful onboarding programs help the new employees develop relationships within the company as soon as possible because relationships help build trust and trust is the core foundation of a great working environment. In this chapter we have slides from eShares, Asana and Valve.

ESHARES

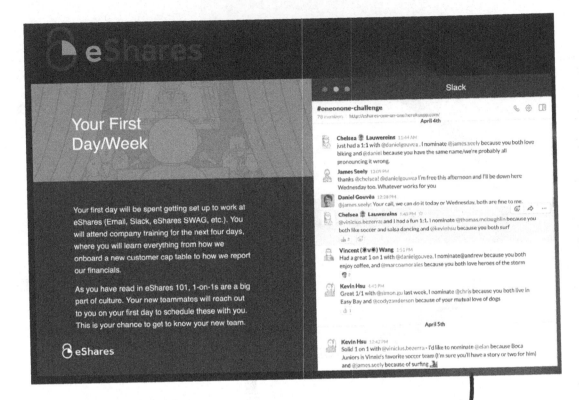

As a new employee, it is natural for you to feel insecure in your new environment; you want to know that the company is organized, that it cares about you, and that its people are prepared for your arrival. You also want to be able to make an impact and demonstrate why you were wisely employed in the first place. This eShares slide does a great job of illuminating the process of getting settled in; it helps to introduce you to your new environment, it sets out the plan (training for the first four days), demonstrates the company's transparency, and mentions that team mates will be in contact to set one-on-one meetings. I really like the clever use of the Slack channel example, which encourages introductions via nominations (including a fun opening remark to start the discussion).

ASANA

Coaching and mentorship

All Asanas are encouraged to <u>participate</u> in a <u>Conscious Leadership Group</u> training, often with several of their team members at the same time. It provides us with a common framework to communicate.

Every Asana has access to executive coaching to work on career and personal development.

We have a robust <u>onboarding program</u> with mentors for every new hire.

Our peer mentorship program facilitates learning amongst Asanas across the entire organization.

TEAM OF PEERS

CULTURE
↓
MISSION
↓
VISION
↓
HISTORY
↓
VALUES
↓
THE WAY WE WORK AROUND HERE
↓
ONBOARDING
↓
DIVERSITY + INCLUSION
↓
FAILURE
↓
TALENT
↓
TRANSPARENCY
↓
FEEDBACK
↓
EMPLOYEE BENEFITS
↓
MAKE A DIFFERENCE
↓
BONUS

In this coaching and mentorship slide, the company Asana makes mention of its robust onboarding program. Having had a look at its website's content regarding onboarding, I think that onboarding deserves a slide all to itself, and I would recommend this to the company. As an example, parts of this quote from the Asana blog *If you want your new engineers to hit the ground running, give them a soft landing* would make for a great onboarding slide. "The first step is to remove as many rote tasks as possible from the new engineer's list of responsibilities. We want him or her to focus on being a member of the organization, not on doing chores. To facilitate this process, we have all of the components of their workstation acquired and set up ahead of time. We give them a $10,000 budget to customize it and then get them what they need before they show up. In the days before their first day of work, we set up their desk, install a standard disk image and run a standard set-up script on their machine. All that's left are the unavoidable personal customizations. The goal of the whole operation is to ensure that the engineer doesn't spend most of their first day "setting up their work-space." We have much bigger plans for them."

VALVE

Your First Day

Fig. 1-1

So you've gone through the interview process, you've signed the contracts, and you're finally here at Valve. Congratulations, and welcome.

Valve has an incredibly unique way of doing things that will make this the greatest professional experience of your life, but it can take some getting used to. This book was written by people who've been where you are now, and who want to make your first few months here as easy as possible.

-2-

Valve Facts That Matter

Fig. 1-2

Valve is self-funded. We haven't ever brought in outside financing. Since our earliest days this has been incredibly important in providing freedom to shape the company and its business practices.

Valve owns its intellectual property. This is far from the norm, in our industry or at most entertainment content-producing companies. We didn't always own it all. But thanks to some legal wrangling with our first publisher after *Half-Life* shipped, we now do. This has freed us to make our own decisions about our products.

Valve is more than a game company. We started our existence as a pretty traditional game company. And we're still one, but with a hugely expanded focus. Which is great, because we get to make better games as a result,

-3-

The Valve deck, as apparently everything else in the company, is done differently than most other such decks. Page 2 alerts new hires that their new environment is going to be very different than other work spaces that they may have experienced previously... "and it can take some getting used to". Valve sets out the basic (and impressive) facts about the company, reminding the new hires about some of the things they will have heard in the interview process.

Personally I really like the way that the company goes on to indirectly compliment the new hires ("[we] recruit the most intelligent, innovative, talented people on earth") and itself, while explaining the flat management-less work environment that these new hires have just joined.

CULTURE
↓
MISSION
↓
VISION
↓
HISTORY
↓
VALUES
↓
THE WAY
WE WORK
AROUND HERE
↓
ONBOARDING
↓
DIVERSITY
+
INCLUSION
↓
FAILURE
↓
TALENT
↓
TRANSPARENCY
↓
FEEDBACK
↓
EMPLOYEE
BENEFITS
↓
MAKE A
DIFFERENCE
↓
BONUS

Your First Month

So you've decided where you put your desk. You know where the coffee machine is. You're even pretty sure you know what that one guy's name is. You're not freaking out anymore. In fact, you're ready to show up to work this morning, sharpen those pencils, turn on your computer, and then what?

This next section walks you through figuring out what to work on. You'll learn about how projects work, how cabals work, and how products get out the door at Valve.

What to Work On

Why do I need to pick my own projects?

We've heard that other companies have people allocate a percentage of their time to self-directed projects. At Valve, that percentage is 100.

Since Valve is flat, people don't join projects because they're told to. Instead, you'll decide what to work on after asking yourself the right questions (more on that later). Employees vote on projects with their feet (or desk wheels). Strong projects are ones in which people can see demonstrated value; they staff up easily. This means there are any number of internal recruiting efforts constantly under way.

If you're working here, that means you're good at your job. People are going to want you to work with them on their projects, and they'll try hard to get you to do so. But the decision is going to be up to you. (In fact, at times you're going to wish for the luxury of having just one person telling you what they think you should do, rather than hundreds.)

But how do I decide which things to work on?

Deciding what to work on can be the hardest part of your job at Valve. This is because, as you've found out by now, you were not hired to fill a specific job description. You were hired to constantly be looking around for the most valuable work you could be doing. At the end of a project, you may end up well outside what you thought was your core area of expertise.

There's no rule book for choosing a project or task at Valve. But it's useful to answer questions like these:

- Of all the projects currently under way, what's the most valuable thing I can be working on?
- Which project will have the highest direct impact on our customers? How much will the work I ship benefit them?
- Is Valve not doing something that it should be doing?
- What's interesting? What's rewarding? What leverages my individual strengths the most?

Freaking out during the first month is OK at Valve, so new hires can relax and just trust that the system will work. The company system requires new hires to pick the projects that they want to work on, ensuring that passion is a key fuel; as they remind their new employees, "you were hired to constantly be looking for the most valuable work you could be doing."

Reading these extracts from the Valve onboarding book is very interesting. Visually, the book has an "old world" feel to it; if you didn't know that Valve is a game development company, you might even think that it was an old fashion magazine. At Valve, the employees are self-directed 100% of the time; Valve's respective self-directive principles seem to have been modelled on the W.L. Gore approach, which advocates that people vote with their feet (or by moving the location of their desk) and the projects that get people signed up (and excited) are the ones that get off the ground. The degree of emphasis on autonomy and self-directed work is impressive and may frighten away many people from the company, which is just fine—and likely a Valve strategy. This company clearly wouldn't appeal to everyone, and that, of course, is part of the appeal; this is not a conventional work opportunity.

Gone are the days when companies didn't have to address issues of diversity and inclusion. These are now non-negotiable areas, and companies have to demonstrate three things: firstly, that they are aware of the various issues facing under-represented or minority groups; secondly, that they are keen to employ individuals from a diverse talent pool; and thirdly, that they (as a company) are willing to learn from their past mistakes in this area. Luckily, this is quickly becoming more than just a tokenistic box-checking exercise; a growing amount of research demonstrates that diverse companies thrive. We're even beginning to realize that neuro-diversity, something that nobody had even heard of ten years ago, is the next frontier in the diversity and inclusion conversation. Diverse companies reflect the society that we live in, and Culture-Driven companies are often at the forefront of building truly inclusive workplaces where people's various skills and qualities can be utilized in a way that empowers everyone and collectively benefits the company.

In this chapter, we have slides from LinkedIn, Hubspot, Asana, Hotjar, and Patreon, each of which demonstrates that inclusive companies create a culture which can positively impact the communities and the wider society that they are all a part of.

LINKEDIN

Diversity: Employee Resource Groups

Inclusion is a core foundation of LinkedIn's culture and our mission. This can only be achieved through a workforce that reflects the rich diversity of our global member base, and this is something we strive to do in all of our hiring efforts.

Diversity is important at LinkedIn, as is clearly exemplified by this slide. It's a core foundation of the culture and the mission of the company, and LinkedIn strives to achieve it in the way that the company hires.

CULTURE
↓
MISSION
↓
VISION
↓
HISTORY
↓
VALUES
↓
THE WAY WE WORK AROUND HERE
↓
ONBOARDING
↓
(DIVERSITY + INCLUSION)
↓
FAILURE
↓
TALENT
↓
TRANSPARENCY
↓
FEEDBACK
↓
EMPLOYEE BENEFITS
↓
MAKE A DIFFERENCE
↓
BONUS

HUBSPOT

> Our goal with diversity and inclusion programming at HubSpot is to create a globally inclusive culture spanning diversity of gender identity, age, ethnicity, nationality, color, sexual orientation, language, perspective, socioeconomic status, thought, and more.
>
> HubSpot

In this slide, it's refreshing to see Hubspot addressing diversity of thought (the lack of which—subtle yet insidious—may indicate how companies aren't *actually* diverse at heart). The big heart clearly communicates the company's intended attitude towards diversity: all are welcome here.

ASANA

Radically inclusive

Our vision for Asana has always included building a diverse team. We see this as <u>critical</u> to creating a culture that attracts the best people in our industry—whether or not they themselves are from underrepresented groups.

Our <u>diversity goals</u> reflect both the culture we'd like to work in and the strategy that leads us to success.

As a company, we strive to be the change we want to see in the workplace. And the workplace we want to see in this world is radically inclusive.

TEAM OF PEERS

The folks at Asana see diversity as a critical component to creating a culture that attracts the best people, no matter what their background is. The company has gone to the lengths of setting up diversity goals and these goals are linked to being the change that Asana wants to see in the workplace, which is to become radically inclusive. The closing paragraph in particular is very powerful, especially the final line.

CULTURE
↓
MISSION
↓
VISION
↓
HISTORY
↓
VALUES
↓
THE WAY
WE WORK
AROUND HERE
↓
ONBOARDING
↓
DIVERSITY
+
INCLUSION
↓
FAILURE
↓
TALENT
↓
TRANSPARENCY
↓
FEEDBACK
↓
EMPLOYEE
BENEFITS
↓
MAKE A
DIFFERENCE
↓
BONUS

HOTJAR

We'll keep this short and simple because to be honest, it's not a complicated subject for us:

> We are firmly committed to providing equal opportunity in all aspects of employment and will not tolerate any discrimination or harassment of any kind. Our team members are encouraged to report any issues or concerns to their team lead or the VP of Operations, and should always remember our Core Values. We also encourage you to review the Acceptable Use Policy of Hotjar Systems.

This is a great slide, especially because the company is acknowledging that the subject of equal opportunity is not complicated—there is, quite simply, a zero-discrimination policy at Hotjar. The slide directs the readers to the company's core values in case of doubt. Overall, the sense I get about Hotjar is that its people mean it when they say that there is no room for discrimination.

PATREON

We build an inclusive environment because we believe that will give us the best chance at funding the creative class.

We fight hard against unfair practices and trends that we see affecting underrepresented minorities at other tech companies.

We want to reverse those trends by creating opportunities for anyone to succeed at Patreon.

CULTURE
↓
MISSION
↓
VISION
↓
HISTORY
↓
VALUES
↓
THE WAY
WE WORK
AROUND HERE
↓
ONBOARDING
↓
(DIVERSITY
+
INCLUSION)
↓
FAILURE
↓
TALENT
↓
TRANSPARENCY
↓
FEEDBACK
↓
EMPLOYEE
BENEFITS
↓
MAKE A
DIFFERENCE
↓
BONUS

Diversity and Inclusion messaging is important to us

There is no such thing as a diverse "candidate" or "person."

Please do not use that language.

"Teams" can be diverse or lack diversity, not individuals.

Also, some teammates prefer gender neutral pronouns. You can find pronoun preference in each person's Slack bio.

If someone slips up and uses improper language, speak up and correct them with compassion. Remember, all feedback at Patreon is KIND and DIRECT.

We put our money where our mouth is when it comes to building a diverse and inclusive environment

- We participate in Project Include.
- We have a program for teammate driven Employee Resource Groups (ERG's).
- We have a Slack channel #diversity to facilitate conversation and information-sharing.
- We have a Diversity and Inclusion Census to collect data that helps us to report on fairness across things like compensation, promotions and other resources. For example, we analytically study performance reviews and look for bias.
- All restrooms are gender neutral at Patreon.
- We apply the lens of diversity to our hiring practices by implementing the Rooney Rule.
- We offer training on topics like unconscious bias, allyship and active listening.
- We built a guide to accommodate people who are visually impaired and people with all ranges of mobility.
- We've audited our benefits to be more inclusive: we've included packages for mental health support, transgender support, as well as conception and fertility packages for all kinds of partners.
- Each team sets inclusivity-based OKRs. We aim to be champions in this space.
- The most important thing is that we do not shy away from tough conversations around diversity and inclusion and, as with all conversations at Patreon, we ask that these conversations are direct and done with compassion. Frequent discourse and debate are key to making progress.

CULTURE ↓ MISSION ↓ VISION ↓ HISTORY ↓ VALUES ↓ THE WAY WE WORK AROUND HERE ↓ ONBOARDING ↓ DIVERSITY + INCLUSION ↓ FAILURE ↓ TALENT ↓ TRANSPARENCY ↓ FEEDBACK ↓ EMPLOYEE BENEFITS ↓ MAKE A DIFFERENCE ↓ BONUS

I really appreciate Patreon's connection to and way of expressing the company's stance when it comes to inclusion. The folks there have really nailed it. It's clear that they are comfortable talking about inclusion, have thought about it in detail, and have developed practices to create a truly inclusive workplace (such as pronoun preferences in Slack). Again, the design is very visually pleasing, as you'd expect from a tech company. I like that these slides are educational as well as instructive. Also impressive is the comprehensive list of ways that Patreon "puts our money where our mouth is" when it comes to diversity and inclusion.

Successful entrepreneurs, when interviewed or quoted, all tend to state that failure is an essential aspect of the journey to success. Some go as far as to say that *failure*—not success—is what they strive for, because failing indicates that you have innovated, taken risks, and stretched beyond your comfort zone. The issue with failing, however, is twofold: firstly, it just doesn't feel good (until and unless you train yourself to recognize it as a sign of eventual success); secondly, lots of company cultures punish failure and only reward success.

Culture-Driven companies are often highly intentional in how they view and frame failure. Failure is featured explicitly in a number of culture decks in order to help potential and current company members rethink what *failure* actually means. In this chapter we have respective slides from Asana, Hubspot, and Soundstripe.

ASANA

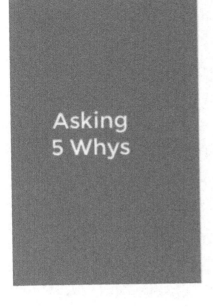

Asking
5 Whys

We treat "failures" as opportunities for growth. When things don't go according to plan, we run a "5 Whys" exercise. By the time we reach our fifth "Why?" we reach the root of the problem and can better avoid the same issues in the future.

I like the way that Asana approaches failure. The company accepts that it will happen and uses the "5 Whys" exercise to dig deeper into the root cause of said failure in order to therefore understand how to avoid failure in the future.

CULTURE

↓

MISSION

↓

VISION

↓

HISTORY

↓

VALUES

↓

THE WAY
WE WORK
AROUND HERE

↓

ONBOARDING

↓

DIVERSITY
+
INCLUSION

↓

⬭ FAILURE ⬭

↓

TALENT

↓

TRANSPARENCY

↓

FEEDBACK

↓

EMPLOYEE
BENEFITS

↓

MAKE A
DIFFERENCE

↓

BONUS

WORK HARD

↓

HUBSPOT

Just because someone made a mistake years ago doesn't mean we need a policy or rule.

WE DON'T PENALIZE THE MANY FOR THE MISTAKES OF THE FEW.

We only protect against big stuff.

Hubspot's approach to failures of the past demonstrates that its folks understand that people can make mistakes. The company has not had a draconian knee jerk reaction to mistakes in the past and guarantees that it will not react so in the future either. The company wants its people to be accountable and take ownership.

SOUNDSTRIPE

CULTURE

↓

MISSION

↓

VISION

↓

HISTORY

↓

VALUES

↓

THE WAY
WE WORK
AROUND HERE

↓

ONBOARDING

↓

DIVERSITY
+
INCLUSION

↓

FAILURE

↓

TALENT

↓

TRANSPARENCY

↓

FEEDBACK

↓

EMPLOYEE
BENEFITS

↓

MAKE A
DIFFERENCE

↓

BONUS

Fail quickly and cheaply.

Adding "and cheaply" to the "fail quickly" phrase implies that a failure shouldn't have a dramatic impact on the finances of the business. This is Soundstripe's expectation: the company leaders apparently know that failure is a necessary step in the learning process, but they still want to mitigate its consequences as much as possible. In order to fail cheaply, the Soundstripe team member should give the potential for failure some thought before making a move, and will need to choose certain proactive parameters that ensure that a failure won't scale out of control and cost the company a lot of money.

We WANT you to try new things and fail at them, because it means progress. You have to fail at things before you succeed. We encourage our team to go out and fail.

Reading that Soundstripe encourages its people to fail because "it means progress" should inspire its ideal candidates to understand that they are expected to learn through attempting tasks, that sometimes they will do them wrong and fail at things, and that it's not only okay—it's a necessary part of the journey.

The only stipulations we have for those failures are:

1. If your idea fails, be self aware and humble quickly move on to the next project.

2. That failure shouldn't break the bank. Test ideas as cheaply as you can. If they work, we can scale them later.

Overall, these slides are inspiring. It's not often that you get told to go out and fail, that the organization you work for *expects* you to not get it right the first time. At the same time, it's reassuring to read that, whether through trial and error or by intentional design, there are two core boundaries in place around the invitation to fail. These boundaries create a level playing field and offer a measure of safety. The Soundstripe culture comes across as genuinely oriented towards innovation, with lots of small, lean experiments taking place.

CULTURE
↓
MISSION
↓
VISION
↓
HISTORY
↓
VALUES
↓
THE WAY
WE WORK
AROUND HERE
↓
ONBOARDING
↓
DIVERSITY
+
INCLUSION
↓
FAILURE
↓
TALENT
↓
TRANSPARENCY
↓
FEEDBACK
↓
EMPLOYEE
BENEFITS
↓
MAKE A
DIFFERENCE
↓
BONUS

TALENT

Over 18m people have read the Netflix culture deck and over 3.8m people have read Hubspot's culture code. That's a lot of talent who after reading those decks know more about whether they might want to work at either company, or not. Company decks should be magnetic – you should either be attracted to what's on the pages or repelled by what you read. If you don't think you would enjoy working in a particular environment that's described in a culture deck you in all likelihood self-select out of the recruitment process. If you really like what you read, you will look to progress with the recruitment process and be well prepared for the interview process. One of the key functions of a Culture Deck is to help attract, recruit and retain the right talent and in this chapter we have excellent examples from LinkedIn, DoSomething, Netflix, eShares, Morey Creative Studio, Nordstrom, Hootsuite, Valve, Patreon, Hubspot, Nanigans and Asana.

LINKEDIN

Jeff Weiner
CEO
Mountain View

Talent is our No. 1 operating priority

LinkedIn uses its CEO in this slide to communicate the number one operating priority for the company: Talent. The take-away message here is that if the CEO says it and advocates it, then the company definitely lives it. It's also an excellent way to put a face to a name, and to thus effortlessly personalize the company while broadcasting a key value.

DOSOMETHING

11 REASONS TO WORK AT DOSOMETHING

1. We've got history
2. We have a kickass staff
3. We love our interns
4. We work hard, but play harder
5. We have a cool crib
6. We're around the world
7. We get around
8. We make campaigns that are big, loud, and easy
9. We have the inside scoop
10. We know all the cool people
11. We're hip and with it

DoSomething covers all the bases for the younger generation with this slide; they talking about loving their interns, working and playing hard, having a cool crib and cool people, and being hip and having the inside scoop. They know how to speak the language of their ideal potential employees, and they prove it here. Millennials should resonate with this slide.

CULTURE
↓
MISSION
↓
VISION
↓
HISTORY
↓
VALUES
↓
THE WAY WE WORK AROUND HERE
↓
ONBOARDING
↓
DIVERSITY + INCLUSION
↓
FAILURE
↓
⬭ TALENT ⬭
↓
TRANSPARENCY
↓
FEEDBACK
↓
EMPLOYEE BENEFITS
↓
MAKE A DIFFERENCE
↓
BONUS

NETFLIX

Great Workplace is
Stunning Colleagues

Great workplace is *not* espresso, lush benefits,
sushi lunches, grand parties, or nice offices

We do some of these things, but only if they are
efficient at attracting and retaining
stunning colleagues

Our High Performance Culture
Not Right for Everyone

- Many people love our culture, and stay a long time
  - They thrive on excellence and candor and change
  - They would be disappointed if given a severance package, but lots of mutual warmth and respect
- Some people, however, value job security and stability over performance, and don't like our culture
  - They feel fearful at Netflix
  - They are sometimes bitter if let go, and feel that we are political place to work
- We're getting better at attracting only the former, and helping the latter realize we are not right for them

CULTURE
↓
MISSION
↓
VISION
↓
HISTORY
↓
VALUES
↓
THE WAY
WE WORK
AROUND HERE
↓
ONBOARDING
↓
DIVERSITY
+
INCLUSION
↓
FAILURE
↓
TALENT
↓
TRANSPARENCY
↓
FEEDBACK
↓
EMPLOYEE
BENEFITS
↓
MAKE A
DIFFERENCE
↓
BONUS

Pay Top of Market
is Core to
High Performance Culture

One outstanding employee gets more done
and costs less than two adequate employees

We endeavor to have only
outstanding employees

Good For Each Employee to Understand Their Market Value

- It's a healthy idea, not a traitorous one, to understand what other firms would pay you, by interviewing and talking to peers at other companies
  - Talk with your manager about what you find in terms of comp
  - Stay mindful of company confidential information

NETFLIX

CULTURE

↓

MISSION

↓

VISION

↓

HISTORY

↓

VALUES

↓

THE WAY
WE WORK
AROUND HERE

↓

ONBOARDING

↓

DIVERSITY
+
INCLUSION

↓

FAILURE

↓

TALENT

↓

TRANSPARENCY

↓

FEEDBACK

↓

EMPLOYEE
BENEFITS

↓

MAKE A
DIFFERENCE

↓

BONUS

Three Necessary Conditions for Promotion

1. Job has to be big enough
   - We might have an incredible manager of something, but we don't need a director of it because job isn't big enough
     - If the incredible manager left, we would replace with a manager, not with a director

2. Person has to be a superstar in current role
   - Could get the next level job here if applying from outside and we knew their talents well
   - Could get the next level job at peer firm that knew their talents well

3. Person is an extraordinary role model of our culture and values

NETFLIX

This combination of slides from the Netflix deck does a great job of communicating how the culture is designed to attract and retain the most qualified and most talented people. The culture is not for you if you "value job security and stability over performance". If you thrive on excellence and candor and change, then Netflix will pay top dollar to employ you if you are the best at what you do; the company is very well aware that the best people get more done and are cheaper in the long run.

Netflix pushes the concept of transparency by encouraging their employees to understand their market value by talking to friends at other companies and even accepting interviews from other businesses. Only a company that is very confident of the magnetic pulling and staying power of its culture would ever encourage its employees to do this. If an employee could potentially earn more at another company, then the manager will know about it and can take action to counteract the situation before it becomes a serious problem. Remember that an outstanding employee costs significantly less in the long run than two adequate employees.

If you want to be promoted at Netflix, then here are three conditions that must be met. Netflix avoids job title inflation with the first condition: "The job has to be big enough". You will not be promoted to Director Level at Netflix just because you have been there for five or fifteen years or you *think* you deserve a promotion, both of which happen often at other companies. If the job is big enough, you will be considered for the promotion if you are a superstar in your current role and could easily step up to the role. You will also only be promoted at Netflix if you are recognised to fully represent the culture and values of the business. If you don't tick all three boxes, there is no point in applying and you may well be headed in the opposite direction…

CULTURE
↓
MISSION
↓
VISION
↓
HISTORY
↓
VALUES
↓
THE WAY
WE WORK
AROUND HERE
↓
ONBOARDING
↓
DIVERSITY
+
INCLUSION
↓
FAILURE
↓
(TALENT)
↓
TRANSPARENCY
↓
FEEDBACK
↓
EMPLOYEE
BENEFITS
↓
MAKE A
DIFFERENCE
↓
BONUS

ESHARES

Why not pay Top of Market?

1. We must earn our talent (we can't "buy" it)

2. The best people deeply value non-financial compensation (often more than financial)

3. Employees that optimize for top-of-market pay are often mercenaries and difficult to align

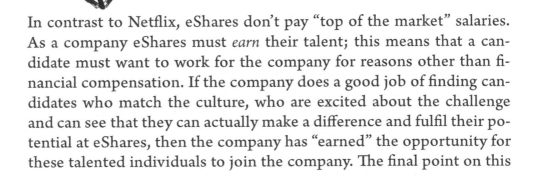

In contrast to Netflix, eShares don't pay "top of the market" salaries. As a company eShares must *earn* their talent; this means that a candidate must want to work for the company for reasons other than financial compensation. If the company does a good job of finding candidates who match the culture, who are excited about the challenge and can see that they can actually make a difference and fulfil their potential at eShares, then the company has "earned" the opportunity for these talented individuals to join the company. The final point on this slide is true: it is difficult to align the candidates that Netflix describes as "mercenaries" (what other companies call "brilliant jerks") with the culture of the company. More importantly, they can invariably be convinced to consider a higher salary elsewhere.

Key Concepts

- Change in responsibility happens before change in compensation (leading indicator)

- However, responsibility and compensation are much more loosely correlated than you would think

- In general, companies are very bad at determining the immediate value of a person at a point in time

- But the market is good at determining the value of a person's career

- Usually Responsibility $\neq$ Compensation at a point in time but...

- The Total Responsibility converges to The Total Compensation over a career (The area under the respective curves)

- To increase compensation, increase responsibility

CULTURE
↓
MISSION
↓
VISION
↓
HISTORY
↓
VALUES
↓
THE WAY
WE WORK
AROUND HERE
↓
ONBOARDING
↓
DIVERSITY
+
INCLUSION
↓
FAILURE
↓
TALENT
↓
TRANSPARENCY
↓
FEEDBACK
↓
EMPLOYEE
BENEFITS
↓
MAKE A
DIFFERENCE
↓
BONUS

This slide does a great job in explaining how the team at eShares think about responsibility and compensation. The more responsibility you want and seek out, and the more responsibility you are prepared to take, the better you will do at the company. Recognition and the resulting increase in compensation may lag after responsibility, but they do catch up over time.

MOREY CREATIVE STUDIO

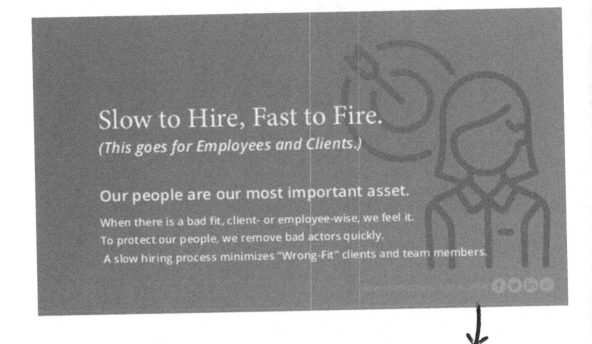

Slow to Hire, Fast to Fire.
(This goes for Employees and Clients.)

Our people are our most important asset.

When there is a bad fit, client- or employee-wise, we feel it.
To protect our people, we remove bad actors quickly.
A slow hiring process minimizes "Wrong-Fit" clients and team members.

I like the fact that, in this slide, the folks at Morey talk about firing their *clients* too—that's not something you often hear. "Our people are our most important asset" further demonstrates that the people in the company are more important than the clients. The company warns prospective employees that the hiring process may be slow, but it ensures a good culture fit between them and the company. If you, as potential employee, are the wrong fit and have managed to slip through the net, the company won't worry for long; "bad actors" are fired fast.

NORDSTROM

It starts with nurturing, inspiring, and attracting **top talent**.

If you want to be the best,
you need to have the best.

TOP TALENT

We use the audition process so that the entire team is involved in quick hiring decisions.

CULTURE

MISSION

VISION

HISTORY

VALUES

THE WAY
WE WORK
AROUND HERE

ONBOARDING

DIVERSITY
+
INCLUSION

FAILURE

TALENT

TRANSPARENCY

FEEDBACK

EMPLOYEE
BENEFITS

MAKE A
DIFFERENCE

BONUS

BRETTON PUTTER

Nordstrom demonstrates how it thinks about top talent in one telling phrase: "if you want to be the best you have to have the best". The Nordstrom recruitment process is handled quickly because its people have developed a full day audition process, which is described in the Hiring Handbook and captures the company's modern mentality about how to attract, vet, and hire amazing people. With its third slide, Nordstrom demonstrates that if you, as a new employee, *do* join the company, you will work on "meaningful challenges" and you will have the opportunity to grow and pursue your potential, knowing that this is a key factor in today's candidates' decision-making process regarding whether or not to apply for or join a company.

HOOTSUITE

Who Thrives at Hootsuite?

✓ People who like to experiment and always try new things.

✓ People who are self-directed and self-motivated.

✓ People who never rest until the job is done.

People who thrive at Hootsuite are passionate, driven, hustlers; entrepreneurial by nature.

CULTURE
↓
MISSION
↓
VISION
↓
HISTORY
↓
VALUES
↓
THE WAY WE WORK AROUND HERE
↓
ONBOARDING
↓
DIVERSITY + INCLUSION
↓
FAILURE
↓
(TALENT)
↓
TRANSPARENCY
↓
FEEDBACK
↓
EMPLOYEE BENEFITS
↓
MAKE A DIFFERENCE
↓
BONUS

This is an excellent slide for potential new hires to understand exactly what the company looks for in a new hire and what is therefore expected of them as employees. The company wants people who are self-motivated and will tackle projects, who are prepared to try new things (and fail, and learn), and who will get the job done no matter what.

Hootsuite is full of driven hustling entrepreneurs who are fuelled by passion: predictably, that is what the company is looking for in new recruits as well.

In the course of researching this document,
we asked dozens of people why they love to come to work.
There were some very common themes that arose:

High Caliber Teammates

At Hootsuite, you get to work with really interesting, smart, open-minded people. They're good at what they do because they're passionate about it.

"When I first came in, I was vibrating with excitement. There was just a certain vibe and you could tell everyone wants to be here, and they're good at what they do and care about their jobs."

Erin Fitzpatrick
Administration Ambassador

Why We Love To Come To Work

Hootsuite

CULTURE

MISSION

VISION

HISTORY

VALUES

THE WAY
WE WORK
AROUND HERE

ONBOARDING

DIVERSITY
+
INCLUSION

FAILURE

TALENT

TRANSPARENCY

FEEDBACK

EMPLOYEE
BENEFITS

MAKE A
DIFFERENCE

BONUS

Many leaders make the mistake of thinking that they can impose a culture on their team, without understanding what their culture really is. These slides communicate that the creation of the Hootsuite culture deck involved not just input from the senior executive team, but from lots of people within the company. This shows considerable consideration and commendable respect of each individual in such a large company. The slides communicate that the people who work at Hootsuite are the type of people you would frankly enjoy working with: interesting, smart, open-minded, and passionate. There's nothing better than being exposed to such a high-energy and passionate environment. Obviously, the more you love something, the better you'll be at it and the more you'll want to pursue it; being surrounded by like-minded people is similarly important, and Hootsuite seems to know and encourage this. Erin's quote on the fourth slide describes these elements of the Hootsuite culture for the reader.

VALVE

Your Most Important Role

Concepts discussed in this book sound like they might work well at a tiny start-up, but not at a hundreds-of-people-plus-billions-in-revenue company. The big question is: Does all this stuff scale?

Well, so far, yes. And we believe that if we're careful, it will work better and better the larger we get. This might seem counterintuitive, but it's a direct consequence of hiring great, accomplished, capable people. Getting this to work right is a tricky proposition, though, and depends highly on our continued vigilance in recruiting/hiring. If we start adding people to the company who aren't as capable as we are at operating as high-powered, self-directed, senior decision makers, then lots of the stuff discussed in this book will stop working.

One thing that's changing as we grow is that we're not great at disseminating information to everyone anymore (see "What is Valve not good at?," on page 52).

On the positive side, our profitability per employee is going up, so by that measure, we're certainly scaling correctly.

Our rate of hiring growth hovered between 10 and 15 percent per year, for years. In 2010, we sped up, but only to about 20 percent per year. 2011 kept up this new pace, largely due to a wave of hiring in Support.

We do not have a growth goal. We intend to continue hiring the best people as fast as we can, and to continue scaling up our business as fast as we can, given our existing staff. Fortunately, we don't have to make growth decisions based on any external pressures—only our own business goals. And we're always free to temper those goals with the long-term vision for our success as a company. Ultimately, we win by keeping the hiring bar very high.

Hiring

Fig. 5-1

The Valve pages regarding *talent* make for a fascinating read. I like that the company has totally turned the whole concept on its head and has created something that requires concentration and time to understand. Valve describes their very different culture and asks and answers the question that's on most people's lips: how does this radically different culture scale? I notice that Valve demonstrates a humble and balanced approach in this document by talking about how profitability per employee is increasing (and "so by that measure, we're certainly scaling correctly") but, at the same time, admitting that they are no longer as good at communication as they were in the past. As a new employee, I would be pleased to read that Valve is not beholden to investors, so the company doesn't experience any external pressure to do something that is not in the company's best interest; in other words, the folks at Valve are masters of their own domain. To scale the business, Valve intends to continue to hire the best people and keep the hiring bar high. This would really resonate with me if I had just been hired by Valve.

Valve flags the focus of the company by saying that hiring well is "the most important thing in the universe!" According to the company, it's more important than breathing; one of the things that new employees should do is to learn how to interview by shadowing experienced interviewers. Valve also has me intrigued because its interview process is different to what most people may be used to if they've been interviewed at previous companies.

Valve understands that the easiest way to influence a company and its culture, both positively and negatively, is through the people it hires. The company doesn't have managers, so the usual checks and balances against hiring the wrong person aren't in place at Valve to the same extent that they are in other companies; a poor hiring decision can cause a lot of damage and can go unchecked for too long. Valve prepares a new hire for the probability of being involved in interviews in the fu-

CULTURE
↓
MISSION
↓
VISION
↓
HISTORY
↓
VALUES
↓
THE WAY
WE WORK
AROUND HERE
↓
ONBOARDING
↓
DIVERSITY
+
INCLUSION
↓
FAILURE
↓
TALENT
↓
TRANSPARENCY
↓
FEEDBACK
↓
EMPLOYEE
BENEFITS
↓
MAKE A
DIFFERENCE
↓
BONUS

ture by supplying a basic three-question check list for evaluating its candidates:

- Would I want this person to be my boss?
- Would I learn a significant amount from him or her?
- What if this person went to work for the competition?

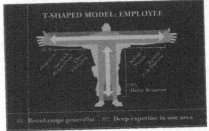

Fig. 5-2

Collaboration is highly valued at the company; for Valve, being able to multi-task while being inventive, iterative, creative, talkative, and reactive, is a combination that's far more important than having domain-specific knowledge or expertise. The company is looking for generalists and experts who are better than the current team and hiring B-level candidates is a terrible mistake that Valve doesn't plan to make.

on temporary/contract help to get us through tough spots, but we should never lower the hiring bar. The other reason people start to hire "downhill" is a political one. At most organizations, it's beneficial to have an army of people doing your bidding. At Valve, though, it's not. You'd damage the company and saddle yourself with a broken organization. Good times!

Hiring is fundamentally the same across all disciplines. There are not different sets of rules or criteria for engineers, artists, animators, and accountants. Some details are different—like, artists and writers show us some of their work before coming in for an interview. But the actual interview process is fundamentally the same no matter who we're talking to.

"With the bar this high, would I be hired today?" That's a good question. The answer might be no, but that's actually awesome for us, and we should all celebrate if it's true because it means we're growing correctly. As long as you're continuing to be valuable and having fun, it's a moot point, really.

– 48 –

Q: If all this stuff has worked well for us, why doesn't every company work this way?

A: Well, it's really hard. Mainly because, from day one, it requires a commitment to hiring in a way that's very different from the way most companies hire. It also requires the discipline to make the design of the company more important than any one short-term business goal. And it requires a great deal of freedom from outside pressure—being self-funded was key. And having a founder who was confident enough to build this kind of place is rare, indeed.

Another reason that it's hard to run a company this way is that it requires vigilance. It's a one-way trip if the core values change, and maintaining them requires the full commitment of everyone—especially those who've been here the longest. For "senior" people at most companies, accumulating more power and/or money over time happens by adopting a more hierarchical culture.

– 49 –

From this page, you can tell that Valve is truly focused on its culture because the hiring criteria are the same across all functions. The only way that you can build a consistent hiring process across all functions is by focusing on the values of the candidates being interviewed. I like the fact that the folks at Valve mention that the design of the company—and the retention of this design–is more important than any short-term business goal.

CULTURE
↓
MISSION
↓
VISION
↓
HISTORY
↓
VALUES
↓
THE WAY WE WORK AROUND HERE
↓
ONBOARDING
↓
DIVERSITY + INCLUSION
↓
FAILURE
↓
(TALENT)
↓
TRANSPARENCY
↓
FEEDBACK
↓
EMPLOYEE BENEFITS
↓
MAKE A DIFFERENCE
↓
BONUS

PATREON

We recruit and retain high-performing and highly compassionate people. You cannot be just one of those things.

We hire people who are actually here to help creators get paid and that's what makes this place really unique.

In our most recent company-wide survey, 100% of our teammates answered "Yes" when asked the question "Is the work that your company does important?"

95% of the company responded that they understand how their individual work directly contributes to the company mission.

We are also externally recognized for our team. The San Francisco Business Times named Patreon one of the top places to work in 2017, and we were named to similar lists in 2016.

People stay at Patreon because they love their teammates and our mission. Our employee attrition rate is ~1/3rd the national average.

We hire and retain world class talent only

When thinking about whom to hire or keep on your team, ask yourself,
"Is this individual world class at what they do?"

Because we hire people who genuinely care about our mission, we can
give more autonomy and trust.

This is why our people decide what they work on.

During company planning, the executive team shares
a vision, strategy, and strategic objectives based on insights and
feedback from the company. From there, our teams decide what they
want to build to support the strategy.

This set of slides is pretty straightforward and powerful—and backed with statistics and facts. They do an excellent job of describing how Patreon works with its people, what the company is looking for in potential employees, and how much autonomy teams have. In the first slide especially, it's noted that high-performing people are often not compassionate, since they tend to put their focus elsewhere and can become extremely demanding of themselves and of others in order to get the job done. Patreon makes it clear that, as a company employee,

CULTURE
↓
MISSION
↓
VISION
↓
HISTORY
↓
VALUES
↓
THE WAY
WE WORK
AROUND HERE
↓
ONBOARDING
↓
DIVERSITY
+
INCLUSION
↓
FAILURE
↓
TALENT
↓
TRANSPARENCY
↓
FEEDBACK
↓
EMPLOYEE
BENEFITS
↓
MAKE A
DIFFERENCE
↓
BONUS

you need to be both—high-performing *and* compassionate—to fit in with the culture.

The story that the second slide tells is readable, engaging, and interesting, and it positions the company—without overtly bragging—as an incredible place to work. The slide explains what makes Patreon unique, why people are motivated to work there, how individuals feel about their ability to make an impact, the awards that the company has won for its performance and culture, and the loyalty exhibited towards the company by its people. The slide focuses on purpose ("is the work that the company does important?") and mission (people stay at Patreon because of its mission and because they feel that their work contributes to fulfilling the mission).

The company hires world-class talent and suggests the simple validation question: "is this individual world class at what they do?" Because those world class high-performers are compassionate and care, they are trusted and receive a lot of autonomy. The executive team sets the vision, strategy, and objectives and the remaining teams decide what they will build to support that strategy. In these slides, Patreon presents itself as a genuinely inspiring and purpose-driven place to work.

HUBSPOT

Culture is to recruiting as product is to marketing.

Customers are more easily attracted with a **great product**.

Talented people are more easily attracted with a **great culture**.

In this slide, Hubspot sets out its thoughts about how important culture is regarding the company's ability to recruit. The parallel that is drawn between product/marketing and culture/talent is extremely helpful. If your company hasn't defined what its culture is, how can you recruit the best people who align with your business? In just the same way, how can you market your product effectively if you don't know what it's made of?

CULTURE
↓
MISSION
↓
VISION
↓
HISTORY
↓
VALUES
↓
THE WAY
WE WORK
AROUND HERE
↓
ONBOARDING
↓
DIVERSITY
+
INCLUSION
↓
FAILURE
↓
TALENT
↓
TRANSPARENCY
↓
FEEDBACK
↓
EMPLOYEE
BENEFITS
↓
MAKE A
DIFFERENCE
↓
BONUS

THERE ARE TWO WAYS TO PROGRESS AT HUBSPOT.

1. Gain mastery as an individual contributor and make magic.

2. Provide spectacular support to those who are doing #1.

Confession: We have a lot of first-time managers at HubSpot. We're working hard to develop them.

The Hubspot formula for progress and success is a simple one. Gain mastery and make magic… or support someone who is doing so and follow in their slip stream as they progress. The "confession" at the bottom of the second slide feels very intentional; the company is proud that it offers people their first opportunity to manage others, yet is also aware of—and is actively tackling—the challenges that inexperienced leadership can create for the company.

NANIGANS

PEOPLE
AT **nanigans**

CULTURE
↓
MISSION
↓
VISION
↓
HISTORY
↓
VALUES
↓
THE WAY
WE WORK
AROUND HERE
↓
ONBOARDING
↓
DIVERSITY
+
INCLUSION
↓
FAILURE
↓
TALENT
↓
TRANSPARENCY
↓
FEEDBACK
↓
EMPLOYEE
BENEFITS
↓
MAKE A
DIFFERENCE
↓
BONUS

BRETTON PUTTER

WILLING
INVESTED
IMPRESSIVE
UNFILTERED
CARING
FUN

nanigans

"Everyone is busy, yet still willing to drop everything to help you out. It's amazing. When someone does that for you, you continue to do it for them – you **pay that forward**. That's our culture. That's the circle of life at **nanigans**."

– Campaign Management

nanigans

Nanigans have, for me, struck gold in these two slides. The reason? The adjectives in the second slide are powerful but they're *not* stuff you hear all the time. They're different, and that grabs my attention. The quote in the third slide speaks volumes about the culture. I particularly like the "circle of life at Nanigans". It says, *yes, it can get pretty hectic working here, but you're not alone, and when you need help, it's always available*. It does seem strange to me—and makes it much less personable—that the quote is attributed to an entity and not an individual person. That said, it's still a really good quote—great energy, great example, with a great sense of compassion. It makes Nanigans sound like a really friendly place to work, while backing up the previous slide's values that revolve around a work hard / play hard mantra.

CULTURE
↓
MISSION
↓
VISION
↓
HISTORY
↓
VALUES
↓
THE WAY WE WORK AROUND HERE
↓
ONBOARDING
↓
DIVERSITY + INCLUSION
↓
FAILURE
↓
TALENT
↓
TRANSPARENCY
↓
FEEDBACK
↓
EMPLOYEE BENEFITS
↓
MAKE A DIFFERENCE
↓
BONUS

ASANA

Recruiting
differently

We take the time to find people who are among the best in the world at what they do or who have the potential to grow into the best. We work as a team to get to know the whole person, communicate our values, and ensure that candidates are well-informed and delighted throughout the recruiting process. But our work extends beyond just our team: our holistic approach to the hiring process involves working with hiring managers, teams, and leaders across the company on everything from our growth plans to our hiring processes and decisions. Recruiting is a company-wide effort and responsibility and we encourage all Asanas to adopt the motto "Always Be Recruiting."

TEAM OF PEERS

I am immediately drawn to this slide because very few companies truly recruit differently. The idea of recruiting "the best in the world" and those who "have the potential to grow into the best" is a bold and inspiring statement, and also indicates that Asana is a company's that's happy to invest in developing people even while it's also open to hiring sure bets. From this slide, it sounds like the folks at Asana don't necessarily hire to fit certain specific roles, but that they perhaps instead focus on bringing the right people on board and then find opportunities for them when they arrive at the company. Terms such as "the whole person" and "delighted" candidates are interesting and encouraging. From the "always be recruiting" slogan, I get the sense that the company is consistently growing and it's everybody's responsibility to be on the lookout for great people who would serve as valuable new additions to the company.

The old command and control, restricted information and share as little as possible model doesn't work in the modern world of business, where trust and speed of decision making are critical. Transparency is not just about sharing information, it's an assurance, as a company leader towards your team and your customers, that your company trusts each employee, at a fundamental level, to do the right thing for the company and themselves. And that assurance—when enforced by reliable follow-up behavior and results that back up that promise—pays off.

In this chapter we have slides from ImAthlete, Patreon, eShares, Hubspot and Morey Creative Studios.

IMATHLETE

BUILD TRUST THROUGH TRANSPARENCY

It doesn't get more straightforward than this, I'd say. ImAthelete's slide emphasizes the word "trust", but the big and bold lettering that is practically bursting through the slide demands that the reader sits up and pays attention. This is the definition of how you foster trust in a company: through transparency.

CULTURE
↓
MISSION
↓
VISION
↓
HISTORY
↓
VALUES
↓
THE WAY
WE WORK
AROUND HERE
↓
ONBOARDING
↓
DIVERSITY
+
INCLUSION
↓
FAILURE
↓
TALENT
↓
(TRANSPARENCY)
↓
FEEDBACK
↓
EMPLOYEE
BENEFITS
↓
MAKE A
DIFFERENCE
↓
BONUS

Transparency

- Open sharing of information

- Honesty

- Regular (constructive) feedback

- It's ok to ask "why?"

- Don't avoid the negative

- Admit when you're wrong

Honesty and transparency make you vulnerable. Be honest and transparent anyway.

Mother Teresa

This slide goes into detail about how the company—in a handful of specific how-to cornerstones—builds trust, upholds honesty, and encourages transparency. The Mother Teresa quote is inspiring, and acknowledges the beautiful yet essential risk of being trustworthy along with emphasizing how important honesty and transparency are despite of—or perhaps, in part because of—this risk.

PATREON

Patreon chooses transparency. However, we should be aware of the potential downsides:

- Key information could leak and damage the company.
- The team could feel information overload via oversharing.
- Information could be misinterpreted without proper context.
- Folks might share problems before having solutions; too much of that could shake confidence in leadership.

Despite these costs, we operate with high transparency to give our team the context they need to make great decisions.

Patreon's leaders approach transparency by first deliberately choosing to be transparent, and then explaining the potential downsides and risks to the company of being transparent.

CULTURE

↓

MISSION

↓

VISION

↓

HISTORY

↓

VALUES

↓

THE WAY
WE WORK
AROUND HERE

↓

ONBOARDING

↓

DIVERSITY
+
INCLUSION

↓

FAILURE

↓

TALENT

↓

(TRANSPARENCY)

↓

FEEDBACK

↓

EMPLOYEE
BENEFITS

↓

MAKE A
DIFFERENCE

↓

BONUS

Here are things we do
to disseminate important information:

- We hold open Q&A at all hands meetings
- The Executive team weekly agenda is public in Asana
- 20% of Executive team meetings are open attendance for the entire company
- All weekly team meetings have public agendas viewable in Asana
- We share board meeting notes and takeaways with the company after each meeting
- All metrics for the business are available in public dashboards
- Data Science and Finance present on company growth and our financial plan every month
- Each time we do a company-wide employee engagement survey, we share results and our actionable next steps
- All team goals are published in a single place and can be tracked by anyone at Patreon

> We will continue to share all of the top-level company information with the team until information is leaked and we cannot. We are yet to have any sensitive information or materials leak.
>
> So long as this is true, we will continue operating this way. There may come a time when we need to change this, but we would like to delay that as long as possible.

They go on to describe how they uphold transparency, specifically listing how the company ensures that relevant information is communicated to its people. Patreon holds the team responsible for transparency, too; if you want it, then you need to respect and uphold it.

Overall, these Patreon slides remind me of the description of how Bridgewater Associates (an exemplary Deliberately Developmental Organization and the world's biggest and most successful hedge fund) operates by demanding "gut-wrenching candor", as sourced from the book *An Everyone Culture: Becoming a Deliberately Developmental Organization*. Granted, Patreon doesn't reach Bridgewater's extent. Nevertheless, such a level of transparency is a pretty rare gem in business, and it's abundantly clear from these slides that Patreon considers transparency to truly be a lived value rather than something which is given lip service. Patreon demonstrates a really sound understanding of the risks of transparency as well as a solid approach to strategizing for the mitigation of these risks. It's truly impressive.

CULTURE
↓
MISSION
↓
VISION
↓
HISTORY
↓
VALUES
↓
THE WAY WE WORK AROUND HERE
↓
ONBOARDING
↓
DIVERSITY + INCLUSION
↓
FAILURE
↓
TALENT
↓
(TRANSPARENCY)
↓
FEEDBACK
↓
EMPLOYEE BENEFITS
↓
MAKE A DIFFERENCE
↓
BONUS

ESHARES

Henry Ward, the CEO of eShares, has written on the company website: "Every month, I send an investor update with our performance, including our income statement and balance sheet. I forward this email to the company so you [referring to all company employees] will see the same information."

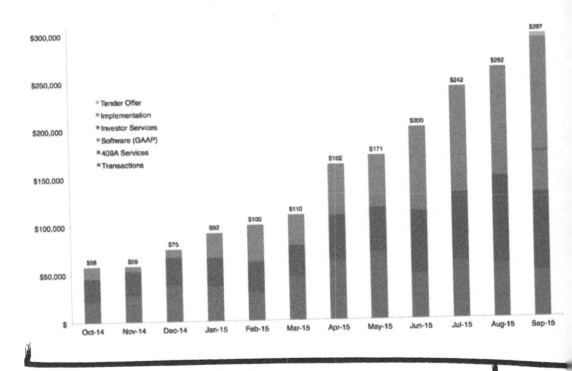

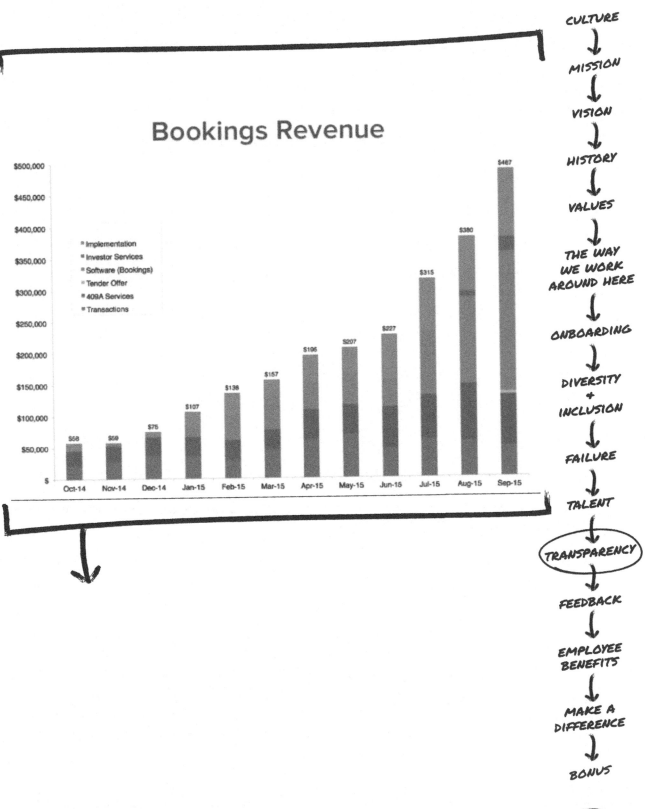

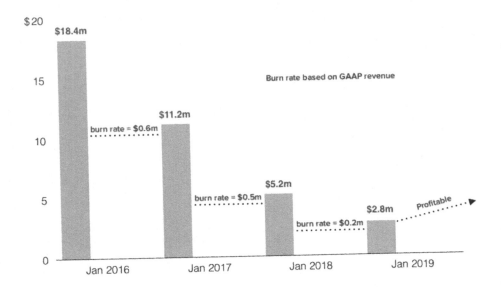

Target 3 Year Net Burn Rate

Burn rate based on GAAP revenue

$18.4m

burn rate = $0.6m

$11.2m

burn rate = $0.5m

$5.2m

burn rate = $0.2m

$2.8m

Profitable

Jan 2016   Jan 2017   Jan 2018   Jan 2019

eShares includes revenue figures in their deck, which clearly demonstrates their level of comfort with transparency in the company. Putting these out in the wilderness of the public eye is certainly a way of "showing" and not just "telling" how this company practices transparency—e.g. in terms of what top management chooses to share with the rest of the employees and the world. The growth that the company has experienced, complimented by the fact that the core software revenues are increasing, is impressive. There is clearly a plan in place; if the company executes on that plan and continues its trajectory, it will achieve profitability in 2019. These are very inspiring slides!

HUBSPOT

3 | We share openly and are remarkably transparent

WE SHARE (ALMOST) EVERYTHING.

We make uncommon levels of information available to **everyone in the company**

(all 1500+ of us, and counting)

WE HAVE THE MOST ACTIVE WIKI ON THE PLANET.*

Examples of things we share and discuss:
- Financials (cash balance, burn-rate, P&L, etc.)
- Board meeting deck
- Management meeting deck
- "Strategic" topics
- HubSpot Lore & Mythology (the funniest page on the wiki)

*Unverified claim

WAIT.
ISN'T HUBSPOT PUBLICLY TRADED?

Yes. We had our IPO in Oct 2014 [NYSE:HUBS]

Usually, publicly traded companies can only share detailed information with a select group of "insiders".

This didn't fit well with our culture. So...

CULTURE
↓
MISSION
↓
VISION
↓
HISTORY
↓
VALUES
↓
THE WAY WE WORK AROUND HERE
↓
ONBOARDING
↓
DIVERSITY + INCLUSION
↓
FAILURE
↓
TALENT
↓
TRANSPARENCY
↓
FEEDBACK
↓
EMPLOYEE BENEFITS
↓
MAKE A DIFFERENCE
↓
BONUS

BRETTON PUTTER

215

> We officially made **every** employee at HubSpot a designated insider.

The Hubspot slide on transparency brings with it the smart, funny tone that has been characteristic of its previous slides. I like the company's chronological story-like design and its overall tone: "Wait. Isn't Hubspot publicly traded?" The vibe or voice of the business is exuded powerfully in this slide; combined with brilliant design, it tells the story of transparency in a clear, memorable way, and it's hard to believe that they would be exaggerating the truth. As a publicly traded company, it *is* a bold move to make everyone a "designated insider", and that serves to make it all the more clear and inarguable that this value genuinely matters at Hubspot.

MOREY CREATIVE STUDIOS

We are Transparent

"Sunlight is the best disinfectant."

Transparent with our clients
All client work is tracked in Basecamp. This provides full transparency into what we are working on, and keeps both sides accountable.

Transparent with our employees
It is better to keep our team members fully informed and involved, and never feeling left in the dark. Nothing good grows in the dark.

Using disinfectant as a metaphor for transparency is a really interesting choice. On the one hand, we can all relate to the image and to the task of cleaning our kitchens and bathrooms; on the other hand, the company is pointing out that there are things that do need to be disinfected. Having said that, the copy on this slide indicates that the people at Morey really do embrace transparency as a value, and they express this in relation to both the company's employees and clients. The links between several characteristics—accountability and transparency; transparency and secrecy—are highlighted well, and overall I get the impression that this company is trustworthy and genuine in its

CULTURE
↓
MISSION
↓
VISION
↓
HISTORY
↓
VALUES
↓
THE WAY
WE WORK
AROUND HERE
↓
ONBOARDING
↓
DIVERSITY
+
INCLUSION
↓
FAILURE
↓
TALENT
↓
(TRANSPARENCY)
↓
FEEDBACK
↓
EMPLOYEE
BENEFITS
↓
MAKE A
DIFFERENCE
↓
BONUS

embodiment of transparency as a value. "Nothing good grows in the dark" really resonates!

FEEDBACK

For lots of people, the question of "Can I give you some feedback?" immediately triggers stress. They get a tense feeling in their chest or stomach and a sense of mild dread. Feedback in business and life is often associated with being criticized; very few people (if anyone) actually enjoy being criticized. As a consequence, many workplaces have unwittingly created cultures where people don't tell each other the hard truths. Sometimes they don't even reflect back on what people are doing well. While this may avoid the short-term pain of having to hear about where you fell short, saving those moments for six-monthly or annual performance reviews which take place behind closed doors creates a bigger problem: a culture where people simply do not thrive and where they never reach their full potential.

There are, however, companies that are doing it differently. In this chapter, we have slides from Next Jump, eShares and Patreon, all of which have created cultures in which feedback isn't just normal, it's expected. So while you're not alone if you balk when you hear the "F" word, you might just come to see it differently if you adopt the practices that are already in place within these ground-breaking companies.

NEXT JUMP

FEEDBACK APP

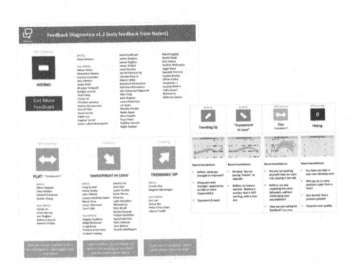

CULTURE
↓
MISSION
↓
VISION
↓
HISTORY
↓
VALUES
↓
THE WAY
WE WORK
AROUND HERE
↓
ONBOARDING
↓
DIVERSITY
+
INCLUSION
↓
FAILURE
↓
TALENT
↓
TRANSPARENCY
↓
FEEDBACK
↓
EMPLOYEE
BENEFITS
↓
MAKE A
DIFFERENCE
↓
BONUS

This slide highlights one of the products that the folks at Next Jump have developed through their culture development initiatives. As the name suggests, the Feedback App is an app to help people provide feedback to their colleagues, which is very fitting for a culture where receiving candid feedback on your potential and also your impediments is believed to be crucial for growing your self-awareness and improving yourself. The app—which facilitates anonymous, transparent, and meaningful communication—looks simple to use. The metrics shown on the right side of the slide are explicit in their descriptions. This company clearly does not hold back in telling people that

a) they're not growing, or b) they're outright hiding and not getting enough feedback from others. It's very encouraging to see that the company's co-CEOs are indicated as growing, and also to note that the company differentiates between those who are "investing in loss," which is seen as a form of growth, and those who are "trending up." It's clear from this slide that feedback isn't just lip service. It is at the very core of what the company prioritizes.

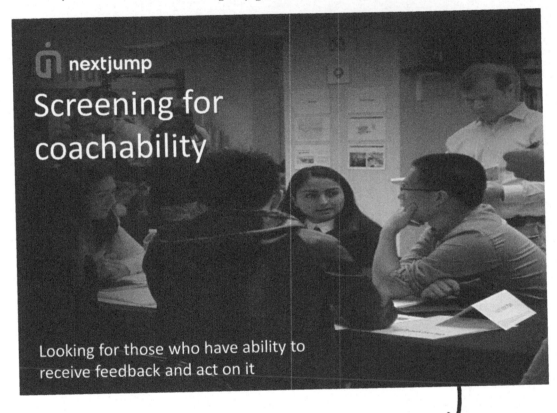

The photograph on this slide is from a Super Saturday recruitment event at Next Jump. During Super Saturday, the company tests candidates for the right "student mindset," a mindset that demonstrates humility and the ability to learn from one's mistakes. Next Jump pays specific attention to how well people receive and then act upon feedback. This is quite different from how talent is identified in lots of other companies, where performance metrics or technical competencies are the focus. The idea of the great importance that this business places on one's ability to take and respond to feedback is fascinating, encouraging, and really quite revolutionary.

CULTURE
↓
MISSION
↓
VISION
↓
HISTORY
↓
VALUES
↓
THE WAY
WE WORK
AROUND HERE
↓
ONBOARDING
↓
DIVERSITY
+
INCLUSION
↓
FAILURE
↓
TALENT
↓
TRANSPARENCY
↓
(FEEDBACK)
↓
EMPLOYEE
BENEFITS
↓
MAKE A
DIFFERENCE
↓
BONUS

Iterate quickly

- Meerkat's frantically dig, but every 20 minutes they stop to look around.

- Stop and ask "am I heading in the right direction?"

- Get feedback early and often

- Everyone waits too long to get feedback. DON'T WAIT.

This eShares slide makes two things very clear: first, that iteration really matters at this company; and, second, that iteration is a natural consequence of getting feedback. The directive about what is expected of employees is extremely clear: get feedback quickly, iterate, and repeat. The cute Meerkat image and its use as a relevant metaphor make the message memorable.

PATREON

If one falls short of our high expectations, they will know about it because we give and receive candid feedback constantly.

We help our teammates through tough times, just as we expect our teammates to stick with Patreon through tough times - to the extent that it serves our mission.

We don't expect anyone to stay with Patreon if we aren't the best way to fund the creative class. And Patreon won't retain someone if having them on our team is not the best way to achieve our mission.

The Patreon values certainly come across in this slide. I like how upfront the company is in stating that times won't always be easy for individual employees and for the company as a whole; it's not all sunshine and rainbows even at the world's most wonderful companies, and the folks at Patreon are mature enough to make note of that. There's great value placed on candid feedback, but it's also clear that persistence and tenacity matter too. Once again, the overriding focus is on the mission: to fund the creative class. That singularity of focus is emphasized in this slide, and it aligns well with the rest of the company's slide deck. I also like the fact that Patreon gives and expects support and loyalty, but also doesn't expect anyone to stay if the company itself isn't living up to its mission of being the best solution for funding the creative class. By the same token, as you can let the company go, if an employee isn't suited to fulfilling the company's mission, he or she will be let go.

CULTURE
↓
MISSION
↓
VISION
↓
HISTORY
↓
VALUES
↓
THE WAY
WE WORK
AROUND HERE
↓
ONBOARDING
↓
DIVERSITY
+
INCLUSION
↓
FAILURE
↓
TALENT
↓
TRANSPARENCY
↓
FEEDBACK
↓
EMPLOYEE
BENEFITS
↓
MAKE A
DIFFERENCE
↓
BONUS

Employee perks are definitely not the definition of a healthy company culture. You will notice, however, that companies with strong cultures do include excellent and extremely thoughtful perks for their employees. Hotjar communicates their mentality on the matter by noting: "Our perks are chosen with an aim to reflect our values and ideals..." and eShares, LinkedIn, and Hootsuite all demonstrate in this chapter how greatly they prioritize their employees' happiness.

HOTJAR

Our Perks

Sara Bent
Last modified Mar 21, 2018 by Ken Weary

Hotjar provides the following list of perks for all of our team members to enjoy. Team members can read more details about using these benefits and allowances by clicking on each link below.

Our perks are chosen with an aim to reflect our values and ideals, be it encouraging constant learning with our Personal Development Budget, a great work / life balance with the annual leave and Holiday Budget, or a happy, healthy team with our Wellbeing Allowance.

Home Office Budget	€4,000/year, topped up €500/year
Personal Development Budget	€500/year
Working Space Allowance	€200/month
Wellbeing Allowance	€200/month
Holiday Budget	€2,000/year
Working Together Budget	€2,000/year
Paid Holiday Leave	40 days/year
Paid Sick Leave	10 days/year
Paid Maternity / Paternity Leave	16 weeks
Company Retreats	2 times/year

New team members are also shipped a special welcome pack when they join our team!

Hotjar entails probably one of the best (if not *the* best) perk system that I have come across. Not just because of what's offered, mind you, but because of the obvious amount of thought that has gone into creating this package. The recognition of maternity *and* paternity leave, the wellbeing and holiday allowances, the company retreats—basically, *all* of the perks listed can be linked back directly to the company's values. This is what all companies should be doing: recognizing that, in order to truly get the best from your people, you need to support them to be healthy, happy, well-rested, and supported individuals. As an exercise, put yourself in the shoes of an executive search consultant working for a company like Hotjar. Imagine the response when you describe the perks to a potential candidate and you tell them that their paid annual leave is 40 days, paid maternity/paternity cover is 4 months and that the company invests over € 9,800 annually in things like your annual holiday budget and your personal development budget. I have experienced this first hand and the candidates are really taken aback. One of the comments I received was, "It is amazing how much thought has gone into these perks. I can see that the company really cares."

ESHARES

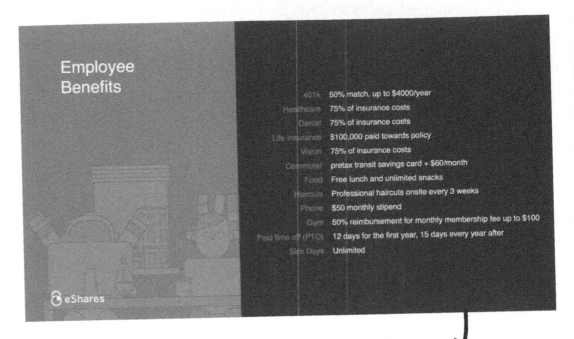

There's a distinctive and even playful vibe to the eShares brand that's evident here: the graphic of the employee with his hands outstretched victoriously in the air and with the rocket on his desk is cute and amusing (he actually looks like an astronaut, and I'm sure there's a good reason for that). The benefits themselves are impressive, covering a range of different areas from pension to healthcare (including dental and vision) and from self-care (including gym, haircuts, and food) to unlimited sick days. This is pretty impressive stuff, and it just goes to show that eShares has definitely put a lot of thought into how they can best support their employees—especially as this is a company that "earns" its employees, and brands itself as a business that doesn't allow high wages to trump the company culture.

LINKEDIN

> **Wellness**
>
> Thoughts, Breathing, Hydration, Nutrition, Movement, and Rest are the six tenets of LinkedIn's Wellness Program. We offer a variety of classes, events and programs to support our employees on their path to greatness.

It's really refreshing to see a company openly acknowledge the power that thoughts, rest, movement, and healthful breathing have (alongside the well-known role that nutrition and hydration play) in promoting our individual wellbeing. I wonder how the phrase "path to greatness" is used across the company and if it has been comprehensively defined? The image of this LinkedIn slide backs up the text by showing a group of LinkedIn colleagues in branded shirts (I like the play on words regarding their logo) at the start of an event which looks like a run or perhaps even a marathon or triathlon.

CULTURE
↓
MISSION
↓
VISION
↓
HISTORY
↓
VALUES
↓
THE WAY WE WORK AROUND HERE
↓
ONBOARDING
↓
DIVERSITY + INCLUSION
↓
FAILURE
↓
TALENT
↓
TRANSPARENCY
↓
FEEDBACK
↓
(EMPLOYEE BENEFITS)
↓
MAKE A DIFFERENCE
↓
BONUS

HOOTSUITE

A Holistic Life

Our quality of life is supported at work. There are things at the office like yoga, fresh juice, organic fruit, dogs, a gym and a nap room—not because it's a gimmick or because everyone is doing it, but because we are already people who pursue a healthy lifestyle and work-life balance.

CULTURE

↓

MISSION

↓

VISION

↓

HISTORY

↓

VALUES

↓

THE WAY
WE WORK
AROUND HERE

↓

ONBOARDING

↓

DIVERSITY
+
INCLUSION

↓

FAILURE

↓

TALENT

↓

TRANSPARENCY

↓

FEEDBACK

↓

EMPLOYEE
BENEFITS

↓

MAKE A
DIFFERENCE

↓

BONUS

The first of these two slides about Hootsuite's approach to wellness is really encouraging. Who doesn't want to work somewhere with yoga, fresh juices, and dogs?! Yes, these things are pretty trendy and perhaps even gimmicky nowadays, but they're also genuinely important for creating a fulfilling, healthy lifestyle. I like the idea of OWLGANIC ALE on the second slide, and the image in the bottom left hand corner is interesting; it reminds me of a school experiment or garden. This slide evokes great characteristics of camaraderie, group activities, and exciting experiments that extent within the company yet beyond the actual *work* space.

Companies that take the happiness of their people seriously look to create an environment where individuals can realise their full potential and self-actualize. The normal issues that arise around employee engagement and retention are eliminated, for the most part, if your employees feel that they are making a difference in the world based on being a part of the future that your company is defining. Nordstrom, LinkedIn, Next Jump and Hootsuite demonstrate that their employees should, and do, have such an opportunity to be the best that they can be while aligning themselves with the company's goals; they are, in essence, encouraging their people to reach their personal potential while contributing positively to something greater than themselves.

NORDSTROM

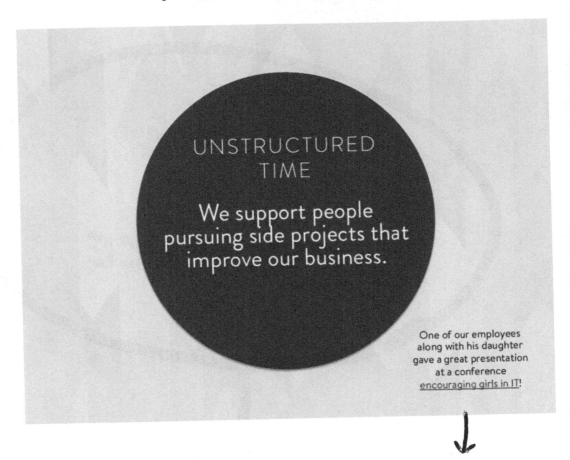

UNSTRUCTURED
TIME

We support people
pursuing side projects that
improve our business.

One of our employees
along with his daughter
gave a great presentation
at a conference
encouraging girls in IT!

This Nordstrom slide made me think "YES!" and I really like the wording and structure they've chosen. Unstructured time is one of the most important initiatives in companies that want to access their people's creative capabilities. I also appreciate the example that is given of the dad and daughter presentation on encouraging girls to get involved in IT.

LinkedIn

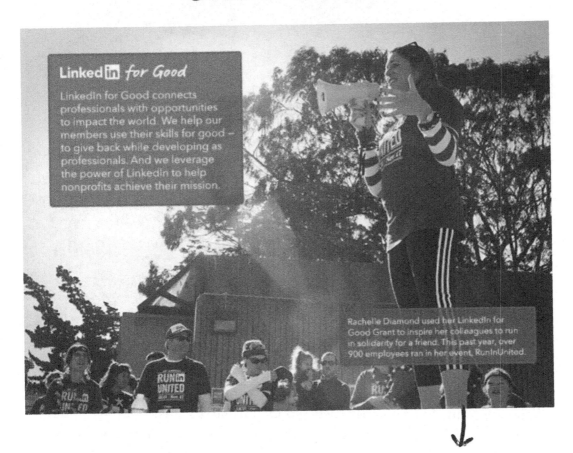

LinkedIn *for Good*

LinkedIn for Good connects professionals with opportunities to impact the world. We help our members use their skills for good – to give back while developing as professionals. And we leverage the power of LinkedIn to help nonprofits achieve their mission.

Rachelle Diamond used her LinkedIn for Good Grant to inspire her colleagues to run in solidarity for a friend. This past year, over 900 employees ran in her event, RunInUnited.

CULTURE

↓

MISSION

↓

VISION

↓

HISTORY

↓

VALUES

↓

THE WAY
WE WORK
AROUND HERE

↓

ONBOARDING

↓

DIVERSITY
+
INCLUSION

↓

FAILURE

↓

TALENT

↓

TRANSPARENCY

↓

FEEDBACK

↓

EMPLOYEE
BENEFITS

↓

MAKE A
DIFFERENCE

↓

BONUS

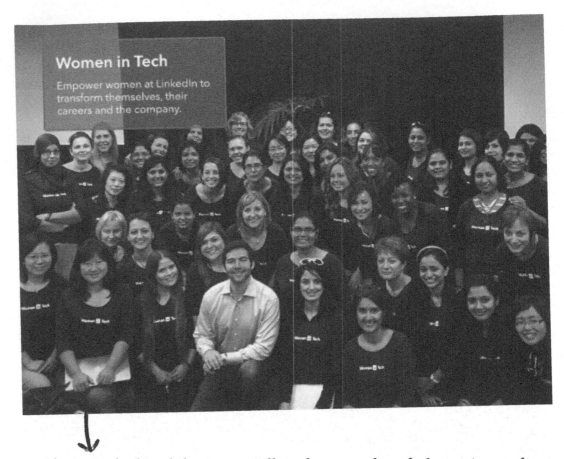

Women in Tech

Empower women at LinkedIn to transform themselves, their careers and the company.

These LinkedIn slides are excellent because they feel genuine and meaningful. The LinkedIn "For Good" initiative, illustrated by the example of Rachelle's "RunInUnited" event, seems brilliant. As a member of the LinkedIn team, you can give back as you personally develop yourself as a professional and as a valuable component of the company. The "Women In Tech" slide showcases diversity in ethnicity and gender, and demonstrates that LinkedIn is at the forefront of trying to solve this major issue in the tech community.

NEXT JUMP

This slide illustrates just how different work is for the millennial generation. Working for a cause rather than an organization is a seismic shift in focus from the mentality of the baby boomer generation. This slide positions how the act of giving back is a central concept at Next Jump. It isn't just a "nice to have" corporate social responsibility project that is bolted onto an organization to make it look good to the outside world; contributing to causes in this way should be, as Next Jump demonstrates here, front and center of an organization's *raison d'etre*.

CULTURE
↓
MISSION
↓
VISION
↓
HISTORY
↓
VALUES
↓
THE WAY WE WORK AROUND HERE
↓
ONBOARDING
↓
DIVERSITY + INCLUSION
↓
FAILURE
↓
TALENT
↓
TRANSPARENCY
↓
FEEDBACK
↓
EMPLOYEE BENEFITS
↓
MAKE A DIFFERENCE
↓
BONUS

HOOTSUITE

We Are Pioneers

We're proud to be at the forefront of the social revolution, a one-of-its-kind company with top talent in the ~~city. country~~. globe.

In this way, we are pioneers. This all contributes to our shared sense of purpose.

"We never set out to build a product that was going to help a protester in Egypt have a voice; it was really about making a good product to help people...it still is."

Paul Donnelly
Principal UX Designer
(and one of Hootsuite's
first 4 employees)

If you are looking to join a company that really does make a difference, then Hootsuite—a company that's at the forefront of the global "social revolution" and that can demonstrate real impact—is definitely to be considered. They emphasize both the company's gradual build-up to its current scale and scope of impact (the globe!) and the distinctive mission that contributes to their shared sense of purpose ("to help people"); this is evident from this slide - from the harmony of their carefully crafted statement to their accompanying and personalized quote by a Hootsuite old-timer.

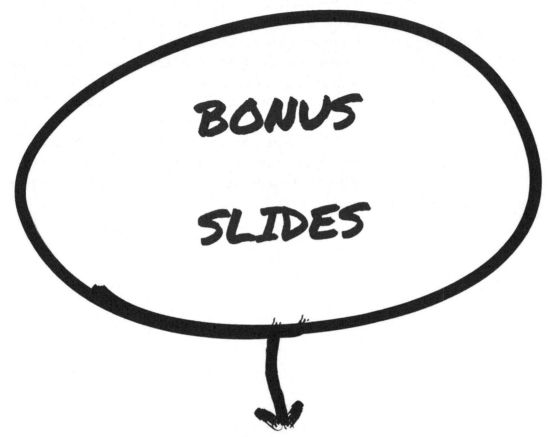

This final chapter consists of slides that are highly effective in getting their message across. These slides from POSSIBLE, DoSomething, Valve, Bizmut, Morey Creative Studios and Hostinger make you think, make you smile or both and demonstrate a deeper level of the company's personality.

POSSIBLE

What's Possible? For context, and according to the company's culture deck: "POSSIBLE is a non-profit that operates in one of the most challenging environments on the planet. In rural Nepal, it is a health care provider for a community of over 260,000 people who live largely without access to electricity, clean water, and basic infrastructure—including roads. The population is still recovering from a civil war that ended almost 10 years ago, the average income is US$150, and the average patient walks 2.5 hours one way to receive care. With all these odds stacked against them, the Possible team has been told their work is impossible hundreds of times, but they've still managed to succeed where others haven't."

11

We believe everything is impossible, until it isn't.

We go to work every day determined to create a better world—to expand humanity's belief about what's possible.

CULTURE
↓
MISSION
↓
VISION
↓
HISTORY
↓
VALUES
↓
THE WAY
WE WORK
AROUND HERE
↓
ONBOARDING
↓
DIVERSITY
+
INCLUSION
↓
FAILURE
↓
TALENT
↓
TRANSPARENCY
↓
FEEDBACK
↓
EMPLOYEE
BENEFITS
↓
MAKE A
DIFFERENCE
↓
(BONUS)

Hope is the belief in the plausibility of the possible as opposed to the necessity of the probable.

—Maimonides

In our team,

HOPE

isn't a fluffy, soft, or naïve concept.

We believe in a hard-edged hope—one created when possibility is earned through execution against all odds.

CULTURE

↓

MISSION

↓

VISION

↓

HISTORY

↓

VALUES

↓

THE WAY WE WORK AROUND HERE

↓

ONBOARDING

↓

DIVERSITY + INCLUSION

↓

FAILURE

↓

TALENT

↓

TRANSPARENCY

↓

FEEDBACK

↓

EMPLOYEE BENEFITS

↓

MAKE A DIFFERENCE

↓

BONUS

BRETTON PUTTER

Do we sound like your kind of people?

Join us to prove possibility.

JOIN US

My reaction to these evocative slides can be summed up in one word: wow. These slides, outlining the company's "hard-edged hope", are genuinely compelling. They are describing a world in which everything is impossible until it isn't, where possibility is created by execution "against all odds." It sounds like the company is attempting and doing important, meaningful, and perhaps even transformative work. The text reminds me of the Margaret Mead quote: "Never doubt that a small group of thoughtful, committed citizens can change the world; indeed, it's the only thing that ever has." I believe that POSSIBLE are.

11

WE'RE COOL AS F*CK 😎

I laughed out loud at this slide. Being *cool* matters to this company and its people are not afraid to show it. It's pretty bold to use "f*ck" and an emoji on a slide, and the brazen choice to do so—alongside the decision to leave a lot of white space—demonstrates that this company is strong in its conviction about being cool. The slide is short and (arguably) sweet, the message is delivered bluntly, and the subtext says: *"It's okay if you have a short attention span. We get it. Now go take a selfie."*

VALVE

Glossary

Jargon. Lingo. Code words.

14-Year-Old Boy—If you see one running your project, don't worry. That's actually 57-year-old Josh Weier *(see Josh Weier)*. If you have any extra stem cells, give them to him! He bathes in them daily.

Australia—A place that's either very near or is New Zealand where more than half of Valve's employees were born.

City of Seattle—Where Valve's founders promised we'd locate our office before pulling a massive bait and switch to the Eastside *(see also Greg Coomer)*.

Coffee Machine, Right-hand Dispenser—The dispenser in all coffee machines at Valve that holds the decaffeinated coffee beans. To the best of our knowledge, these have never needed to be refilled. For all we know, the beans are decorative plastic.

Company Vacation—Every year, the company gathers all the employees and our families, flies us somewhere tropical, and gives us a free weeklong vacation. Popular pastimes include beard contests, snorkeling, ice cream socials, jet skiing, or just sitting on the beach chatting with the locals about how many googly-eyed seashells you should buy from them. (Your feeling: none. Their counteroffer: Just buy five then.)

Empty Shelf on Fifth Floor—Place we're planning on putting all those awards for *Ricochet* once the gaming world finally catches up with it.

Fishbowl—The conference room by the lunchroom. The one with a big glass wall. Don't let the name throw you—we don't actually use it as a fishbowl! Except, of course, on Fishbowl Fridays, where we fill it up with ten thousand gallons of putrid saltwater so that all the manta rays and sharks will have something to breathe while they fight to the death. You won't see it in your list of benefits, not because it isn't fun, but because it is illegal.

Freight Elevator—*(See "Method to move your desk," on page 18.)*

Gabe Newell—Of all the people at this company who aren't your boss, Gabe is the MOST not your boss, if you get what we're saying.

CULTURE → MISSION → VISION → HISTORY → VALUES → THE WAY WE WORK AROUND HERE → ONBOARDING → DIVERSITY + INCLUSION → FAILURE → TALENT → TRANSPARENCY → FEEDBACK → EMPLOYEE BENEFITS → MAKE A DIFFERENCE → BONUS

If you are going to create a different deck, do it with the panache of Valve. As with all the Valve slides, this one demands sustained attention and focus, but luckily the copy is so funny and well-written that I don't want to skim it or skip it altogether. The humor in the company comes across like ten thousand gallons of putrid seawater, and there is a lot of good information here about the company culture. Even the decision to put a glossary in their culture book is revealing (and, yes, entertaining). Some of the jokes, such as those that name actual people, are clever because they will become funnier once a new joiner has gained a bit of experience in the company and gains more context; other jokes give titbits of information about the company's history, benefits, and day-to-day office life (such as it being clear that no one here drinks decaf!). A paid for company vacation for everyone and their families is a bold move—it really tells you that leadership hires people they would want to go on holiday with (quite literally). I also like the way they use the empty shelf on the fifth floor to deal with failure.

BIZMUT

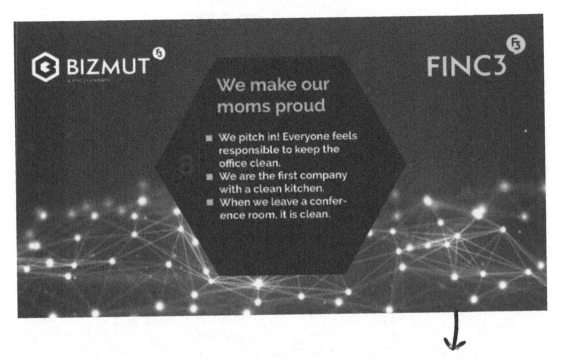

Kitchens in startup offices are often an appalling mess. Bizmut doesn't hire cleaners, though. Instead they make their moms proud and do all the cleaning themselves; therefore, they are (and this is tongue-in-cheek) the first and only company in the world with a clean kitchen, and it's not just their kitchen but their conference room too. The slide communicates that the company culture is fabricated with a delightful sprinkling of humor combined with pride and a sense of ownership and responsibility over the company.

CULTURE
↓
MISSION
↓
VISION
↓
HISTORY
↓
VALUES
↓
THE WAY WE WORK AROUND HERE
↓
ONBOARDING
↓
DIVERSITY + INCLUSION
↓
FAILURE
↓
TALENT
↓
TRANSPARENCY
↓
FEEDBACK
↓
EMPLOYEE BENEFITS
↓
MAKE A DIFFERENCE
↓
BONUS

MOREY CREATIVE STUDIO

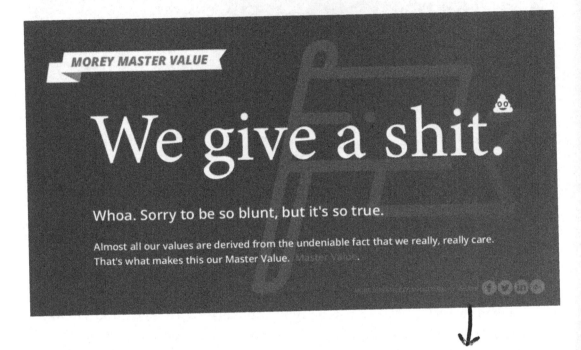

This slide also made me laugh. It also made me nod in understanding. To take the poo emoji and make it white, seemingly using it as an asterisk after the bold, blunt statement of "we give a shit" is funny, unusual, and bold. The tone is conversational yet persuasive. I believe them. I believe, from this slide, that—above all—Morey cares. In fact, as the folks there say, they "really, really care". The repetition of "Master Value" (three times!) on the slide makes the phrase hard to miss. I like the idea of *master value*; it's different and communicates the overarching principle that guides and informs the entire culture and business at Morey. The humor balances the depth of compassion nicely; without it, there would be a risk that Morey could come across as just a bit too earnest or even corny. Thanks to their shitty sense of humor, the company doesn't.

CULTURE

↓

MISSION

↓

VISION

↓

HISTORY

↓

VALUES

↓

THE WAY WE WORK AROUND HERE

↓

ONBOARDING

↓

DIVERSITY + INCLUSION

↓

FAILURE

↓

TALENT

↓

TRANSPARENCY

↓

FEEDBACK

↓

EMPLOYEE BENEFITS

↓

MAKE A DIFFERENCE

↓

BONUS

HOSTINGER

Discuss, Agree/Disagree, **Commit**

We encourage discussions and constructive feedback. Every opinion is important and is likewise challenged. We vocally express disagreement in the manner of constructive criticism and choose not to maintain pseudo harmony in the team. Once a decision is made, we commit wholly and together work towards the goal.

This slide, outlining Hostinger's three part "Discuss, Agree/Disagree, Commit" process reminds me of Next Jump's "Meet, Vent, Work" process for their Talking Partners strategy. It's clear from the text (and visual) that this is a company culture where challenging conversations are embraced rather than avoided, and where unity emerging from turbulence is valued higher than "pseudo harmony" (which, as the name describes, isn't real harmony at all). The Hostinger culture comes across as strong and mature. I think the company has struck a good balance between welcoming individual input and working together towards a common goal. You get the sense that there is a mature level of tolerance for uncomfortable (but necessary) conversations that you perhaps wouldn't find at most other companies.

NEXT JUMP

nextjump

Recognition

Crowd sourced recognition focused on servant stewardship

Programmes:
Consistent: Coronitas and Top 10
Intense: Avengers

This is a heartfelt image and not one that you see in most culture decks. Next Jump's culture of servant leadership and helping others is reinforced through the company's emphasis on recognizing team members for their achievements. The company has three different types of rewards, which differ in consistency and intensity: weekly Coronitas, monthly Top 10s, and annual Avenger awards. Coronitas is the weekly ritual of giving thanks to others, which happens every Friday at 5pm. At Coronitas, a Next Jumper can call someone out for helping them that week and reward them with a baby Corona beer. The monthly peer-voted Top 10 event is meant to celebrate employees who have helped others to succeed that month. The annual Avengers event celebrates the top servant leaders, as voted by the entire company. The winning Avenger is celebrated at a company get-together in

CULTURE
↓
MISSION
↓
VISION
↓
HISTORY
↓
VALUES
↓
THE WAY
WE WORK
AROUND HERE
↓
ONBOARDING
↓
DIVERSITY
+
INCLUSION
↓
FAILURE
↓
TALENT
↓
TRANSPARENCY
↓
FEEDBACK
↓
EMPLOYEE
BENEFITS
↓
MAKE A
DIFFERENCE
↓
BONUS

New York where his or her parents are flown in as a surprise to celebrate the occasion... as pictured on this slide.

ESHARES

1 - 1s

- Every 2-3 weeks with your direct manager

- Go for a walk. 30-40 minutes.

- Have fun. This is your time.

- Talk about what's on your mind. Doesn't have to be work related.

🔗 eShares

What do I talk about during 1-1s?

- Complaints. Get it off your chest.

- Successes. Brag about yourself.

- The weekend. What are you doing?

- Questions. What random question have you wanted to ask?

- Anything that is on your mind. It is all fair game.

CULTURE

↓

MISSION

↓

VISION

↓

HISTORY

↓

VALUES

↓

THE WAY
WE WORK
AROUND HERE

↓

ONBOARDING

↓

DIVERSITY
+
INCLUSION

↓

FAILURE

↓

TALENT

↓

TRANSPARENCY

↓

FEEDBACK

↓

EMPLOYEE
BENEFITS

↓

MAKE A
DIFFERENCE

↓

BONUS

What does the manager do in 1-1?

- The manager's rules for 1-1s are:

- Shut-up and listen

- Seriously. Shut-up. Even if it is awkwardly silent.

- Do not offer advice, feedback, or lessons. Do not ask for it either.

- Just get to know the person you are talking to

I really like how, with these slides, eShares keeps up the casual and camaraderie-fostering vibe. It also offers a pleasant alternative to a situation that most employees have learned to dislike: the one-on-one meeting. One-on-ones can be notoriously ineffective, dull, and are often dreaded; the company has decided from the get-go that it is going to try to make such meetings less structured, more casual, more fun, more personalized, more regular, and more active.

WHERE TO START

My recommendation, if you are beginning to think about developing your culture, is that you start by working with your team to understand and define what your core values are. Your values, just like human DNA, are the definitive building blocks of your company's culture. Once you've created a list of values that you care about and resonate with, you can take the next step of defining the expected behaviors associated with those values. The expected behaviors can then be embedded into business processes such as interviewing or onboarding, which in turn will start to help you define "the way we work around here". Once you have your values and expected behaviors defined you can move on to defining your vision, mission and the other pieces of your culture deck that you choose as relevant for your business.

Culture is not currently recognized as a business function in the way that sales and finance are, however the market is shifting, and I believe that in the next five years we will see culture management become a critical leadership discipline and business function. If you are starting out on the journey of defining your company culture and crafting a culture deck, remember your culture changes with your business. The way your company operates with 10 people will not be the same as with 50 or 200, and your culture deck needs to be kept up to date, as the business's processes, policies and procedures change. If you approach your culture deck as an ever-evolving business function dashboard, you will be taking your first steps towards meeting the future head on.

ABOUT MY FORTHCOMING BOOK THE CULTURE GENE: LEADERSHIP AND CULTURE DEVELOPMENT LESSONS FROM HIGH-GROWTH COMPANIES

9 out of 10 CEOs fail to leverage the one competitive advantage that they have complete control over. The 10% of CEOs who do maximize their culture automatically gift themselves with a powerful asset and an above-average chance of success.

When culture is ignored or neglected, it remains invisible, subconscious, and intangible—with tangible results. A non-prioritized culture can evolve into a dangerous liability that hinders all efforts to grow the business. Without a well-defined company culture, multi-billion-dollar businesses like Airbnb, Spotify, Atlassian, Slack, and Pinterest could not have scaled so spectacularly and sustainably.

The CEOs profiled in The Culture Gene don't just invest in their culture; they use it as the cornerstone of every business decision, aligning behavior with the company's core values, mission, and vision. Prying open the invisible black box of high-growth company cultures, this book delves deeper into the inner workings of culture to explain exactly what it is, how it works, and why it matters for you.

Among of myriad of other examples, strong company culture is also:

- Why Unbounce was able to save $1.5M annually on recruitment fees…
- How Makers Academy enables all its employees to set their own salaries…
- How Hotjar scaled a fully remote business (from $0 to $10M ARR, from 4 to 57 people) in three years…
- Why Influitive holds a 9-minute daily Sync Up meeting that's mandatory for its 180+ employees…
- Where Skimlinks decided to position the office toaster…
- Why Next Jump has a "no fire policy"…
- When a business can use a dragon bouncy castle as a means of evaluating a candidate's culture fit…

Made in United States
North Haven, CT
14 December 2021

12730251R00154